DOES IT
FREEZE?

FAMILY MATTERS

DOES IT FREEZE?

BRIDGET JONES

WARD LOCK

To Neill, my freezer organizer

First published 1991 by Ward Lock
Villiers House, 41/47 Strand, London WC2N 5JE, England

A Cassell imprint

© Ward Lock Limited 1991

Typeset by Columns Design and Production Services Ltd, Reading
Illustrations by Tony Randell
Printed and bound in Great Britain by Collins

British Library Cataloguing in Publication Data
Jones, Bridget
  Does it freeze?
  I. Food.   Home deep freezing
  I. Title   II. Series
641.453

ISBN 0–7063–6960–2

CONTENTS

INTRODUCTION

The freezer is more than a super larder, it provides one of the best methods of preserving food. Taking the freezer for granted may mean that we don't use it to full advantage. Making notes and testing for this book certainly jolted me into freezer-sense.

Being enthusiastic about food personally as well as frequently testing numerous recipes for publication, I make diverse use of my freezers. Unusual items from specialist shops, cooked dishes and certain ingredients prepared in advance for major cooking sessions are all frozen. Seasonal produce, gluts of apples and welcome gifts from other gardens are also preserved safely. We always have bread, butter and something for supper, along with some cake for making a good trifle, tucked away.

This may make me sound like the type of super-organized person who usually infuriates me. However, the tips that follow are based on experiences, many relating to my own bad planning. By trial and error, I have discovered that some foods will out-live their recommended freezer life without causing disaster; others do go rancid.

After a long day testing recipes, I've sometimes packed away an unlabelled cooked dish, convinced I'll know what it is when needed a few days later. Once, I popped a lidded foil container into the refrigerator to thaw before an informal supper party. The contents (a sort or ratatouille, I thought) were due for transformation into a gratin-style starter, but an hour or so before my friends arrived I discovered I had thawed some chicken curry. What an occasion to test creative culinary resourcefulness!

The information and hints in this book may help you to avoid disasters and inspire you to make the best possible use of valuable freezer space. Happy blanching and packing!

BUYING AND SITING
A FREEZER

Rushing out and buying what seems to be a bargain is certainly not the way to acquire a freezer. Forethought and planning are particularly important when buying a freezer, possibly more so than with other kitchen appliances. The two main points to consider are where you intend to put the freezer and what you want to use it for. Then start looking at the different types of freezer that are available and assessing how well they suit your requirements.

Finding a Place for the Freezer

There is no point in thinking about buying a vast chest freezer if you do not have a suitable place in which to put it. So, first have a good look around your home for the right place to put a freezer. It must be kept in a dry place near a power point. Damp and condensation will cause the outer cabinet to rust over a long period and may affect other components. Ideally, the freezer should be in a cool place and there must be space around it for air to circulate. There must also be sufficient space for opening the door or lid of a chest freezer and for removing the drawers from an upright freezer. Here are a few notes on possible different locations.

Kitchen Many upright freezers are designed to be fitted into a kitchen but this is not a good place to keep a chest freezer. A small kitchen which gets quite hot is not ideal for any freezer but if this is the only space you have, then look for a suitable upright model.

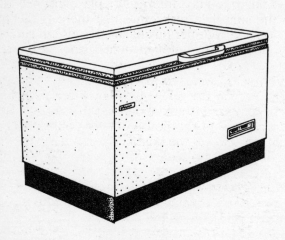

A chest freezer is not a good choice for a kitchen, mainly because this type is best in an unheated area. It also requires more floor space than an upright model and its lid must be kept clear for access. More space may be needed to one side of a chest freezer for efficient ventilation, making it difficult to slot it into the usual arrangement of fitted cupboards and other appliances.

If you are positioning an upright freezer or fridge-freezer in the kitchen, then plan to put it as far away as possible from any equipment that gets hot.

Spare Room A spare upstairs room may be suitable for the freezer provided that it is cool enough, allows space around a chest freezer and is well ventilated. Any central heating radiators should be turned off to keep the temperature down. Never plan to disguise a freezer by putting it in a cupboard or by covering it with curtain-like drapes.

Conservatory Although an unheated conservatory may be the perfect place for a chest freezer in the cold of winter, this is far too hot an area when the sun shines. If you do have to put a freezer in a place that gets quite hot in the sun, then make sure that there is plenty of ventilation and consider buying a fan to use in summer.

Utility Room An unheated utility room is the ideal place for a freezer and when next to the kitchen, this also allows easy access to frozen food.

Garage A clean, dry garage is a good place, particularly for a chest freezer. Think about ease of access – if the garage is linked to the house, this is unlikely to be a problem but if it is at the bottom of the garden, perhaps it is not a practical place.

Types of Freezers

There are three options: a chest freezer, an upright freezer or a fridge-freezer.

Chest Freezer This has an upward-opening lid (page 13). A separate fast-freeze section is a usual feature. Some food may be kept in the special baskets which hang from the top of the cabinet.

The advantage of this type of freezer is that it will hold a lot of frozen food. When the lid is opened there is minimum loss of cold air. Long or unusually shaped items, such as whole French loaves, may be stored in a chest freezer.

The depth of the freezer can be a disadvantage. A person of average height may find bending to reach food in the farthest corner a bit tedious; a short person may not be able to reach right down towards the back of a chest freezer.

Arranging food can be more difficult in a chest freezer and it is more necessary to keep a record of the contents with this type of cabinet to avoid forgetting out-of-date packs.

Upright Freezer This type of freezer has a front-opening door which on many models may be hinged either on the right or left to suit individual requirements. The food is stored in wire or polythene drawers. Some models have shelves with flip-down fronts.

This appliance is more suitable for putting in a kitchen or where floor space is at a premium. It is easier to organize the contents by using the drawers to store different types of food. However, it is necessary to make sure packs are of the right shape and size to fit into the drawers. Some unusually shaped rigid containers may not fit, or some tall ones (for soup and other liquids) may not stand upright.

Fridge-freezer This combines a refrigerator and freezer in two separate sections in the same appliance. Depending on the model, the refrigerator may be at the bottom or the top and it may be larger, smaller or of equal size to the freezer compartment. A fridge-freezer is ideal for the home which does not have enough space for two separate appliances, and where the freezer has to go into a small kitchen. It is also ideal for a small family. However, when looking at a fridge-freezer do make a critical assessment of your needs and don't forfeit refrigerator room for freezer capacity.

Features to Look For

✳ ✳✳✳ Make sure that the freezer has this star marking which means that it is suitable for both the long-term storage of food and freezing fresh food.

Controls Look carefully at the controls, making sure that there is a fast-freeze setting with an indicator light to remind you that it is on. Make sure the controls are in a position where you can see and adjust them easily; perhaps you may want a freezer with controls that are out of the reach of children. Some freezers have a warning light to let you know of any malfunction which needs attention.

Thermometer   Some freezers have built-in thermometers so that you can check the internal temperature
easily. Make sure the thermometer is positioned so that
it is easy to read.

Interior Light   A useful feature in a chest feeezer,
particulary if the appliance is in a poorly lit area.

Well-fitting Drawers   In an upright freezer, look for
drawer fronts that fit neatly to keep in as much cold air
as possible when the door is open.

Split-opening Upright Freezers   Very tall upright
freezers are available with two doors. This means that
you can open just one section at a time, making for
maximum retention of cold air when removing or
adding items.

Lockable Lid   Make sure that the lid of a chest freezer
has a lock. This is particularly important if there are
children in the household or if the freezer is to be kept
in an unlocked garage where intruders may remove
food. Check too that the freezer lid may be opened from
the inside if you are worried about the possibility of
children climbing into the cabinet.

Drainage Hole   Some chest freezers have a drainage
facility for defrosting.

Assessing Your Needs

On the whole, this is the most difficult part of buying a
freezer. Often, cost is a major factor. It is not terribly
practical to think of all the ideas you have for using a
freezer if your bank balance clearly dictates your choice.
If finding the cheapest option that provides the most
space is the key issue, then consider that chest freezers
tend to be slightly cheaper than upright ones with
similar capacities.

If your budget is more flexible and your main
concern is to buy an appliance that is neither too small
nor too large, it is a good idea to make a list of your
reasons for owning a freezer.

☆ If your main reason is to buy and store frozen foods, then think about how much you consume over a set period. To get some idea of the bulk, think about the number of packs of frozen vegetables you would need to store for, say, three months.

☆ You may want to freeze batches of home-grown produce.

☆ Once-monthly shopping trips for key items may be the object.

☆ Buying bulk packs of certain foods may be your aim.

☆ You may want to store lots of ready-made dishes, either home-made or bought.

☆ Buying meat in bulk may appeal to you.

☆ You may want to take advantage of pick-your-own farms.

Generally, most people want to use the freezer for a variety of reasons, although it is true to say that those with large gardens or with access to fresh produce locally may primarily want to use it to store seasonal foods.

When you have made a list of possible uses, combined with some idea of how much frozen food you already consume without a freezer, then you can make an assessment of how large an appliance you need. Remember that once you purchase a freezer you have invested in an appliance which has little secondhand value compared to the original price, so think big rather than small.

Shopping Around

Have a good look around specialist freezer shops, department stores and electrical suppliers. Look at the appliances which your friends have and ask them how practical they find them. Seek expert advice from qualified sales staff. In a large store, ask to speak to someone who is qualified to give advice. By law assistants should not mislead you – this can be important if, for example, you want an appliance to go into a warm kitchen, without breaking down.

Gather literature and information on individual appliances to study at home. Ask whether there are any instruction leaflets for display appliances so that you can study them briefly while in the shop.

Taking Delivery It is important that freezers are handled correctly to avoid damaging them in transit. They should not be tilted at acute angles from their working position. Once in your home, follow the manufacturer's instructions closely for turning on the power. Usually, the freezer should be allowed to stand for a few hours after moving and before operating to allow the oil in the compressor to settle.

When you take delivery of an appliance, check that you do not sign a form which says that the freezer is working properly. Until the appliance has been allowed to settle and it has been turned on for a few hours, you will not know whether it is working properly or not. If you do sign, then write 'received but not inspected or checked'.

Secondhand Freezers As with any secondhand electrical purchase you take a chance. You should be shown a freezer that is in use and working satisfactorily. Check that the outside is in good condition and that the door seals properly when shut. Be careful if you are considering a freezer which is not in use. Moving the appliance can ruin it, so take care (page 17).

Before Using the Freezer

Read the manufacturer's instructions and follow them. Wash out the inside of the freezer with a solution of bicarbonate of soda in warm water – about 2 tablespoons soda to 1.75 litres/3 pints water. Leave the freezer open to dry thoroughly before switching it on. Allow it ot reach the correct storage temperature (−18°C/0°F) before freezing food. Check the temperature with a thermometer.

DEFROSTING

Most chest freezers need defrosting annually; upright freezers should be defrosted twice a year, except those which have automatic defrost. Again, always read and follow the manufacturer's instructions.

Use a plastic scraper (supplied with the freezer) or a soft kitchen spatula to remove any build-up of frost periodically. Plan to defrost the freezer in cold weather. Frozen food will thaw more quickly in summer and the freezer will take longer to reach the working temperature again after defrosting.

Think ahead about the contents – either run them down or arrange to store the food in another freezer. Alternatively, pack all the food together in a neat block in a large polythene bag, then wrap it in lots of newspaper and blankets to keep the cold in. Put it in the coldest possible place.

Never apply a source of heat to the freezer to defrost it quickly. This can permanently damage the cabinet. Similarly, do not use a sharp implement to scrape away ice as you could damage either the pipework or the cabinet.

A bowl of hand-hot water may be placed in the freezer to speed up the thawing process. One bowl may be placed on each shelf of an upright freezer. Place some newspaper on the floor in front of an upright freezer to catch any drips. Gently scrape away the ice with a plastic scraper as soon as possible.

Wash the freezer out with a solution of warm water

and bicarbonate of soda (page 15), then make sure it is completely dry. Turn the freezer to the fast-freeze setting and replace the frozen food. Remember to turn the fast-freeze setting off when the required running temperature is reached ($-18°C/0°F$).

Moving House

The best possible idea is to run down freezer stocks so that the appliance may be switched off and defrosted before moving. Otherwise, think ahead and arrange to store frozen food in friends' freezers or ask your butcher if you have one.

If you cannot avoid moving a freezer full of frozen food, then be sure to warn the removal company in advance and also remind the men who turn up on the day. Make certain they know the freezer must be the last item into the van and first off.

Pack the food into large, heavy-duty polythene bags in the freezer. Lift the bags out so that the freezer may be carried to the removal van, then put the bags back into the cabinet and shut the door or lid. Make sure the food is not forgotten in a corner on the floor once the empty freezer is in the van (this really happened to us!). Carrying a freezer full of food is not practical – the weight may also damage the base of a chest freezer. Once it reaches its destination, leave the closed freezer for an hour or two (depending on how long it has been in transit) for the oil to settle before switching it on.

IN AN EMERGENCY

If there is an unexpected loss of power or if the freezer breaks down, there are a few points to remember.

☆ In the event of a breakdown, check that it is not caused by a fused plug or that the switch has not been accidentally turned off. If the fuse in the plug has blown, replace it and have the appliance examined by an electrician to find the cause of the fault. Check that the socket is working by plugging in another appliance.

☆ The freezer cabinet is insulated to keep in cold air so the food is not going to thaw immediately.

☆ The fuller the freezer, the longer the contents will take to thaw.

☆ If there is a lot of space in the freezer, pack it quickly with crumpled newspaper. Have the paper already crumpled before opening the door and do this speedily to prevent loss of cold air.

☆ Do not open the lid or door of the freezer. Keeping the door shut will conserve the cold air.

☆ Covering the top of a chest freezer with a thick, folded blanket helps to keep in the cold. Remove it again when the electricity supply is restored.

☆ The contents of a full freezer which is left unopened should stay in good condition for 24 hours. Opening and shutting the door to check the contents will cause them to thaw more quickly.

Handling Thawed or Part-thawed Food

Remember, food does not instantly go off if accidentally thawed. As a general rule, if the food is still hard after a freezer breakdown, then allow it to re-freeze, using and eating it promptly. Uncooked meat and poultry may be cooked in casseroles, sauces and similar dishes, then cooled and frozen as for cooked dishes. Similarly, thawed raw fruit should be cooked and frozen; vegetables may be made into soup and frozen; pastry should be rolled out, used and cooked, then frozen for short periods. This is all better than wasting the food, even if the end result is not ideal.

Food that is completely thawed should be used up within 24 hours. Ice creams and similar items should be used while still firm or discarded. Most thawed cooked food will keep in the refrigerator for up to 24 hours. Baked items and bread will keep as for day-old baking.

Common-sense rules of food safety and hygiene ought to be applied. If food is long thawed (by hours, I mean, not days) and beginning to look, smell or feel unacceptable, then it should always be discarded.

Freezer Insurance

Special insurance policies are available to cover freezer contents in the event of loss. Read the policy carefully. Notify the insurance company immediately in the event of prolonged breakdown. In the event of a claim you may have to keep the thawed freezer contents for a specified period for the insurer's inspection.

Check any house contents policy which you have as some do contain a clause covering freezer contents.

FREEZING EQUIPMENT

A section on equipment seems to suggest that once you have a freezer, you need a whole range of accessories. This is not true but it is important to use the correct form of packaging. In addition, you will need 'equipment' for blanching food; a well organized kitchen will usually have suitable utensils.

For Blanching

Two main items: a large saucepan and a basket. The saucepan should be made of stainless steel, glass or enamel-lined. Avoid aluminium and copper. If you intend processing large quantities of fruit and vegetables, then it is worth investing in a huge, double-handled catering pan together with a basket of corresponding proportions. Find a local catering equipment supplier in the telephone directory or a good cookshop should be able to order a suitable pan.

Buy a basket to suit the saucepan. A large, new deep frying basket will do for most large saucepans. In fact, a large, new deep frying pan with a basket is a good buy.

In addition you do need a large bowl (full of iced water) in which to cool the blanched vegetables. If you are confident that your sink, when thoroughly scrubbed out and rinsed, is acceptable, then fine.

For Packing
There is an enormous variety of packing materials and equipment on offer, from those sold in supermarkets to the even greater choice in larger hardware shops and the more diverse items available from specialist suppliers. The following is a quick run-through of the different forms of packing.

Polythene Bags   Probably the most practical form of wrapping. Use only heavy-gauge bags for wrapping food which is to be frozen; thin bags do not protect the food sufficiently and they tend to rip easily.

For packing liquid foods, or other foods which do not hold their shape, in bags, first line a rigid freezer container with a bag. Then ladle in the food and seal the bag. Place the container and bag in the freezer until the food is hard, the lift the polythene pack from the container for storage.

Polythene Tubing   Available from specialist suppliers, this is a roll of flattened polythene tubing, ready to make bags of any length. For neat bags with flattened corners

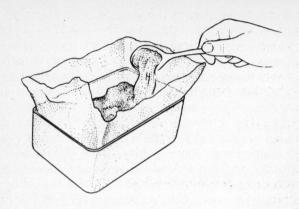

a heat sealer should be used; however, the tubing is also ideal for storing several portions of food or identical items. Cut the required length of tube and tie a firm knot in one end. Place a portion of food minced meat, for example in the tube, then extract as much air as possible and tie another knot. Keep adding the portions to the tube, excluding air and tying knots. The resulting chain of items keeps the same food items together.

Self-sealing Polythene Bags   These have a polythene strip sealing device along the opening. They are useful for large packs of foods which have been open-frozen as they can easily be opened for removing part of the contents and closed again.

Colour-coded Polythene Bags   Heavy-gauge polythene bags with identifying strips of colour on them. Useful for quick identification of different types of food or for organizing the contents of a chest freezer easily.

Batching Bags   Large, coloured carrier bags in which to store similar packs of food. I use clean carrier bags brought home from supermarkets and they work equally well.

Interleaving Film   Lightweight polythene film which is rather like a polythene tissue. Sold in sheets or in perforated rolls, this is not intended for wrapping food but for separating items that are stacked or paired.

When removed from the freezer, items separated by film may still be firmly frozen in a block. Usually, the best way to separate them so as to remove the required number is to bang the edge of the 'block' of items firmly on a clean work surface.

Cling Film   Ordinary weight cling film is not strong enough to protect food which is to be frozen. It is useful for interleaving some foods. It is also useful for excluding air from around foods. **Note** Following recent government recommendations, do not use cling film with high-fat foods such as cheese, pastry or rich biscuit dough. Use interleaving film instead.

Polythene and Foil Bags   Known as 'lami foil' bags, these are polythene-lined foil bags with square-gusseted bases. They stand firmly upright, making them useful for filling with sauces, stews and so on. They are usually sold with wire fasteners and when packed they keep a neat shape. They are, however, expensive.

Boilable or Freeze-cook Bags   These are designed to go straight from the freezer into boiling water or for use in the microwave. If they are to be used in the microwave, then they should be sealed with polythene, microwave-proof ties. They are useful for small portions of vegetables, cooked rice and other cooked dishes that may be reheated successfully from frozen. The bags should be placed on a dish if they are put in the microwave and the fastening loosened very slightly to allow steam to escape.

Roasting Bags   Too fragile for freezer use.

Foil   This is sold in different weights; the lighter foil is not suitable as a freezer wrapping. In general, even the thicker gauge foil is not the best packing material to use, since it does not seem to protect the food as well as polythene in the long term. I find it useful as a wrapping for oddly shaped foods, such as joints, which are then put into polythene bags. If the initial wrapping of foil is tightly closed around the food, it helps to exclude air.

Foil is also useful for tenting over delicate items that are kept in the freezer for short periods of up to a week, when they will survive without correct wrapping.

Foil Containers In all sorts of shapes and sizes, often with cardboard lids. Cooked casseroles and other foods which are to be reheated when thawed may be packed in foil containers, sealed with the lids and frozen. The container of food may be thawed unopened in the refrigerator, then placed in the oven for heating through. When packing in foil-lidded containers, the cardboard side of the lid should have the contents written on it and it should be put on the pack, foil side down.

Rigid Polythene Containers Be sure before buying, that they are recommended for use in the freezer. Some inferior containers do split easily. If you have complied with the recommendations, do not feel bashful about complaining to the shop about any containers which do not withstand freezing.

Lidded containers have the advantage of being easy to stack and label but they are expensive and large quantities of them can present a real storage problem when they are not in use. Reserve them for more delicate casseroles containing beef olives, chicken joints and so on.

Rigid containers that contained yogurt and similar bought items may be used after being thoroughly washed and dried. Since they are not designed for freezer use, once the food is in them and the lid in place, they should be sealed in a polythene bag.

If you are in doubt about whether the lids on rigid containers seal properly, secure them in place with freezer tape.

Ovenproof Glassware Containers A range of oven-proof glass dishes complete with special lids to cover them while in freezer use. Expensive but versatile and useful for short-term storage of prepared dishes.

Freezer to Oven Ware   Many ranges of baking dishes are sold for use in the freezer, microwave or conventional oven. They are particularly versatile even though they are an expensive option.

Always check how they should be used before buying. For example, are they suitable for use **in** the freezer, microwave and oven or can they be put straight **from** freezer to oven? Some dishes which separately withstand both extremes of temperature, will not survive the sudden change in temperature.

Freezer to Hob   Saucepans, casseroles and so on in ovenproof glassware designed for use on the hob. These are reasonably priced and withstand the temperature shock when transferred straight from freezer to heat. The practicalities of buying a significant number of such dishes to keep them in the freezer for long periods is questionable. Useful in the short term.

Freezer Tape   Strong slightly stretchy sticky tape designed specifically to go in the freezer. When using it to seal containers, stick the tape firmly to one point on the rim, then pull it around the rim, stretching it slightly as you go. By stretching the tape it shrinks back tightly against the container, fitting neatly into the join between lid and container to form a lasting airtight seal. A good buy.

Polystyrene Trays   Do not use these in the freezer. Polystyrene is an insulating material which keeps heat in and cold out (or vice versa). It increases the time taken for the food to freeze.

Vacuum Pump   A useful gadget for removing air from bags, this looks like a balloon pump but works in reverse.

Wire Twists   Usually sold with packs of polythene bags, paper- or polythene-covered wire strips to twist around the ends of bags.

Microwave-proof Ties Polythene strips that form a band around the end of a bag. For food which may be thawed or reheated in the microwave. Loosen the tie slightly before putting in the microwave to allow steam to escape.

Polythene Clips For closing bags, these are re-usable and available in two different widths.

Labels Just make sure they are large enough to hold all the information you want to include. To save time, when freezing batches of the same food, put all the packs in a large bag and just label that. Keep it closed to avoid losing unidentified items.

Optional Extras

Freezer Knife or Saw A large-toothed, serrated cutting blade heavy enough to saw through frozen foods. Heavy freezer saws, obtainable from some catering suppliers, may also be used to cut frozen meat. Some electric carving knives have special freezer blade attachments.

Freezer Mitt An insulated mitt (or glove) rather like an oven glove. Designed for handling frozen food.

Storage Baskets Although most chest freezers are sold with at least one storage basket, additional baskets can be useful for stacking in the freezer as well as for sitting on the rim. Always check that they fit into the freezer before buying.

Polythene Trays White polythene trays with shallow rims are available in different sizes from most hardware shops. They are useful for open-freezing food instead of using metal baking sheets.

Washing Tongs A pair of old-fashioned wooden washing tongs is useful for reaching packages at the bottom of a chest freezer. Keep them hanging near the freezer.

FREEZER RECORD

Keeping a freezer record sounds like living in an ideal world but it need not be a time-consuming task. The idea is to list items as you put them into the freezer and to cross them off as you take them out. When you intend taking out certain types of food, you should check your list to see which pack should be used first. To work in this way, the list must give the date on which a pack was frozen, concise details about its contents and the date by which it should be used. Ideally, hang the list near the freezer so that you can refer to it on each occasion you add or remove a pack.

I have to admit that I do not keep a proper freezer record, mainly because so many of my visits to the freezer are made in a tearing hurry when we still haven't had dinner at 9pm. What I do firmly recommend are periodical freezer sort-outs and list-making, bringing items that need using up quickly right to the top. Anything that is for immediate use gets put into a basket to be consumed within days. Then we list all the cooked dishes that should be used, in the order in which they ought to be eaten. I find this system works well – for a few weeks at least we conscientiously cross off items as they are taken out. Even if I do not have a detailed record of all the freezer holds, I am aware of the contents. The pitfall to avoid is to leave all the freezer contents totally unexamined so that ancient packets of

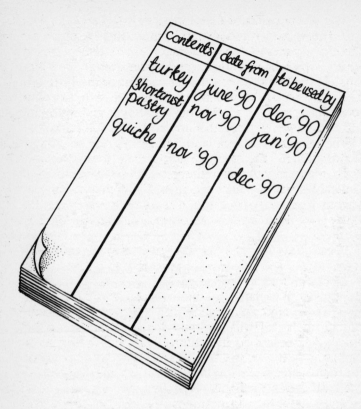

contents	date from	to be used by
turkey	june '90	dec '90
shortcrust pastry	nov '90	jan '90
quiche	nov '90	dec '90

food, months and months overdue for eating, linger in the farthest corner.

Out of Date Food Packs

The suggested storage time for frozen food is a guide to the period within which there will be no loss of quality. The extent to which food deteriorates after the suggested life depends on its type. The important point to remember is that if the food is frozen, even if it is well past the suggested storage life, it is not going to be potentially hazardous to health.

The worst result of over-long freezing is rancidity in fats. This is most noticeable in bacon, which turns rancid after comparatively short storage. It can also occur in turkey which has greatly exceeded the storage life – but this depends entirely on the fat content of the bird and is limited to any fat which lies under the skin. Coconut which is stored for a long time also tends to develop an 'off' taste, even in cakes that are stored for long periods.

The majority of fruit and vegetables, on the other hand, endure long storage without deteriorating badly. Even many months after they should have been used, vegetables will be quite acceptable if slightly lacking in flavour or colour. Fruit, too, if used for cooking can be quite good long after the recommended storage life has expired.

Bread does not taste 'off' after extended storage but it tends to be dry. The same applies to some cakes.

If you do find an ancient package in your freezer, the best advice is to thaw it in the refrigerator and inspect it. If it has a high fat content which may have become rancid, then this will be immediately apparent by the smell, best described as a strange, almond-like aroma. A similar taste becomes more distinctive with the extent of the deterioration. Cooked dishes that have developed such 'off' tastes are usually best discarded for reasons of palatability. Food which smells fine should be cooked quickly and used. Combining vegetables with sauces tends to disguise poor texture and careful seasoning can mask a weak flavour.

AN A-Z OF FREEZING NOTES

A

APPLES

Apples freeze well for use in cooking; they do not freeze well for eating raw as they lose their crisp texture. Cooking apples are usually frozen but cooked eating apples are also successful and may be thawed for making flavoursome pies, fools and so on. Apples discolour very quickly once they are peeled, so it is best to prepare them in quantities that you can process quickly.

Preparation Peel, core and slice the fruit. Plunge it immediately into a bowl of cold water which has a good squeeze of lemon juice added.

Blanch For 1–2 minutes.

Pack Pack, seal and freeze the dried apple slices immediately. They may be packed dry, without sugar, or sprinkled with sugar. Record the quantity of suger used in the pack on the label. Alternatively, the fruit may be packed in syrup (page 118), but slices sprinkled with sugar are easier to separate when frozen.

Ascorbic acid (page 34) may be added to prevent discoloration if necessary; however if the fruit is handled speedily, this should not be necessary. Some apples turn brown more quickly than others; adding ascorbic acid is useful for those that discolour quickly. Lemon juice may be used instead but you have to add it in such quantities that the apples will have a lemon flavour.

Storage Time   Apples keep well for up to a year or longer.

Use   If possible, cook the fruit from frozen or a part-frozen state. For example, when making a sauce or stewing fruit, put the apples in a saucepan over low heat. Sprinkle in sugar as required. Break up blocks of apple slices as they thaw. Check the fruit frequently, keeping a lid on the pan the rest of the time. Add just a little water if necessary.

If you want to use the fruit uncooked, for example in pies, crumbles or in a savoury stuffing, then leave it in a covered container at room temperature until half-thawed. Allow at least 2–3 hours.

Microwave Note   Apples may be cooked from frozen in the microwave. Transfer to a suitable covered container and break up a block as it thaws. To thaw apples in a microwave, allow about 8 minutes on Defrost setting for 450 g/1 lb fruit.

APRICOTS

It's worth freezing fresh apricots when they are available at a reasonable price, for use later in pies and other cooked puddings. The thawed fruits tends to be soft, making the skin seem tough, so they are not ideal for using uncooked. Select fruit that is just ripe and still firm.

Preparation   Wash, dry, halve and stone the fruit. The best way to do this is to make a cut around an apricot into the stone, then twist the two halves firmly, but gently, apart. Submerge at once in syrup (page 118) which has ½ teaspoon ascorbic acid or the juice of 1 lemon added to each 600 ml/1 pint.

Pack   As soon as the fruit is prepared, pack it in rigid containers. Leave a little headspace (page 77). To keep the fruit submerged in the syrup, put a piece of crumpled greaseproof paper on top of it before fitting the lid.

Storage Time   Up to a year.
Use   Use the fruit from frozen and cook very gently in a covered saucepan, stirring occasionally. Add when frozen to pies and other puddings, allowing a little extra cooking time.

Apricot Purée

This is by far the best way of freezing fresh apricots. Cook the fruit with a little lemon juice, then rub it through a sieve. Sweeten the purée if you like. Cool and pack in a rigid container, leaving a little headspace (page 77), then note on the label whether or not the purée is sweetened.

Sweetened purée is perfect for mousses, fools, ice creams, cold soufflés, and to make sweet sauces. Unsweetened purée may be used to make hot soufflés (added sugar would make the recipe unbalanced) and in savoury sauces as well as for sweet recipes.

ARTICHOKES, GLOBE

These may be frozen whole or with the leaves removed just leaving the bottom (or *fond*).
Preparation: whole   Thoroughly wash the artichokes. Trim away the tough outer leaves and stalk ends, and snip off the leaf tips.
Blanch   For 8 minutes in a huge pan of boiling water, with the juice of a lemon added. Drain, cool rapidly and drain well. Dry on absorbent kitchen paper.
Pack   In pairs in bags, removing as much air as possible. Seal and label.
Storage Time   Up to 1 year.
Use   Plunge frozen artichokes into boiling water, with salt added, if liked. Bring back to the boil and cook for 12–15 minutes.
Preparation: bottoms   Prepare the artichokes as above, then cook them in boiling water until tender – about 20 minutes, depending on size. Pull off a leaf to check if the vegetables are cooked – it should come off

easily. Drain well and plunge into iced water to cool the vegetables. Pull off all the leaves, then discard the hairy choke. Trim the bottoms neatly and pat them dry on absorbent kitchen paper.

Pack Wrap individually in cling film, or stack with layers of interleaving film. Pack in bags, with the air removed, in a safe place where the bottoms will not get crushed. Alternatively, pack in rigid containers.

Use Place on absorbent kitchen paper on a plate to thaw. Cover and leave at room temperature for 2 hours or in the refrigerator for 4–5 hours. Alternatively, the artichoke bottom may be stuffed and baked from frozen. Good hot with garlic butter, or a herby breadcrumb stuffing. May also be used cold in salads.

ARTICHOKES, JERUSALEM

Like potatoes, these do not freeze well raw; however, they are good cooked and mashed or puréed, in soup or in gratin-type ready-prepared dishes.

Preparation Peel the artichokes and put them in water with a squeeze of lemon juice added immediately. Simmer the prepared vegetables in salted water for 10–20 minutes, depending on size. Drain the artichokes well, then mash, sieve or purée them until smooth. Do not add butter or additional seasoning at this stage – it's best left until the vegetables are to be served.

Pack In rigid containers or bags with a little headspace (page 77).

Storage Time About 6–9 months.
Use Thaw at room temperature for several hours or in the refrigerator overnight. Beat the vegetable well and reheat in a covered dish over boiling water or in the oven. Mix in a knob of butter and seasoning to taste, with a little milk or cream. Snipped chives, chopped parsley or grated nutmeg may be added to taste. Alternatively, season the mashed artichokes, top with a mixture of fresh breadcrumbs and grated cheese, and bake until golden.

The thawed mashed or puréed artichokes may be used in soufflés, vegetable terrines or combined with some potato as a delicately flavoured topping for meat, lentil or vegetable mixtures (cottage-pie style).

ASCORBIC ACID
Available from chemists in tablets or powder form, ascorbic acid, or vitamin C, may be used to help prevent discoloration in fruits such as apples. It is more effective than lemon juice, which also imparts its own flavour to the fruit. Dissolve in a little water just before use.

ASPARAGUS
Freeze tender, young asparagus spears. Tough stalk ends or spears may be frozen as soup or to flavour a sauce.
Preparation Wash and dry well. Trim off tough stalk ends.
Blanch For 2 minutes. Do this in a special asparagus cooking basket in a deep saucepan, or lay the spears flat in a deep frying pan, fish kettle or large flameproof casserole.
Pack Dry the spears on absorbent kitchen paper before packing them in a rigid container. Open-freezing is a better method for large quantities. Cover a baking sheet with cling film. Lay out the asparagus in a single layer, cover with more cling film and freeze. As soon as

it is firm, pack the asparagus in bags, remove all the air, seal and label.

Use Cook the asparagus from frozen, allowing about 5–7 minutes in the minimum of boiling, lightly salted water.

Asparagus Sauce Base

Cook ½ finely chopped small onion in butter until soft. Add 225 g/8 oz prepared, cut up asparagus and 600 ml/1 pint stock (chicken, veal or vegetable – note which one on the sauce base label). Season lightly and simmer, covered, for 20 minutes. Purée in a blender, sieve and cool. Freeze, allowing headspace (page 77).

Use Chicken, meat, fish or vegetables may be cooked in the sauce base. It may be thickened by adding it to a roux (25 g/1 oz flour cooked in 25 g/1 oz butter) and bringing to the boil, then simmering for 3–5 minutes. Beurre manié (page 40) may be whisked into the sauce base to thicken it. Alternatively, it may be thickened by adding egg yolks and cream, then heating gently without boiling. Taste and adjust seasoning before serving.

Asparagus sauce is good with fish, chicken, turkey, veal and vegetable dishes such as a terrine.

AUBERGINES

In my opinion, the texture of thawed aubergines is poor. It is better to freeze slices as part of a dish – moussaka without its topping – or in ratatouille if it's to be reheated and served hot.

AVOCADOS

Whole avocados do not freeze well as they become rather watery. When they are very plentiful, good quality and cheap, it is worth mashing the flesh with plenty of lemon juice and freezing it for short periods.

Pack In small rigid containers so that the avocado thaws quickly.

Storage Time   Up to 2 months.

Use   Thaw and use in dips or sauces. Mix the mashed avocado with mayonnaise, soured cream, Greek-style yogurt or fromage frais to make a delicate dip. Add snipped chives or a little chopped spring onion for flavour. Also good for making guacamole.

FREEZER TIP   Make a quick chilled avocado soup by combining part-thawed mashed flesh from 2 avocados with 150 ml/¼ pint cold chicken stock in a blender. Stir in 300 ml/½ pint milk and 300 ml/½ pint single cream, yogurt of fromage frais. Stir in a little chopped mint or plenty of snipped chives. Serve at once.

Avocado Parfait

This is a really rich, very easy ice cream. It will keep for 4–6 weeks but it is best eaten with a couple of weeks. In a blender or food processor, combine the flesh from 4 avocados with the juice of 2 lemons and 100 g/4 oz icing sugar. Fold in 300 ml/½ pint whipped whipping cream and 2 teaspoons chopped fresh mint. Freeze until two-thirds frozen (this usually takes a few hours), then blend or process the parfait until smooth and re-freeze it until firm. Put the container in the refrigerator for about 20 minutes before serving.

Use slightly less icing sugar and add 2–3 pieces preserved stem ginger (chopped) and about 4 table-spoons green ginger wine (for example 'Crabbies') to give the parfait a kick, if liked.

B

BACON

Both bacon rashers and joints freeze well for short periods; keep them for too long and the fat does taste rancid.

Preparation Wrap bacon rashers in quantities that you can use easily in cling film, then in a polythene bag.

Joints should be tied in a neat shape, ready for cooking, and sealed in a polythene bag. Bacon cubes are best open-frozen (page 93) or frozen in small packs.

Storage Time Rashers will only keep for 4–6 weeks, depending on the salt and fat content. Bacon which is cured by a traditional method must be used within 4 weeks as the salt and fat content makes it go off quickly. Vacuum-packed bacon with a lower salt and fat content tends to keep a little longer.

Joints may be stored for up to 2 months.

Use Single bacon rashers may be cooked from frozen. Thaw larger quantities for several hours in the refrigerator. Thaw joints overnight in the refrigerator.

Bacon Bits

Trim off and discard the rind and excess fat from the edge of streaky bacon, then dice it. Cook the bits in a heavy-bottomed frying pan over a medium heat, stirring often, until evenly browned and really crisp. Drain on absorbent kitchen paper. Cool, pack and freeze. Use from frozen as the bits thaw quickly. Toss them into salads or with pasta, olive oil and garlic (add fresh basil too!). They keep for up to 2 months.

BANANAS

These do not freeze well – they turn black and mushy.

Banana Freeze

Mash 4 ripe bananas with the juice of 1 lemon. Beat in 6 tablespoons honey until the mixture is really smooth. Add 300 ml/½ pint Greek-style yogurt and mix well. Freeze until half-frozen, then beat the mixture well or work it in a food processor. Freeze again, beat once more, then freeze until firm. Leave in the refrigerator for 15 minutes before serving. Store in the freezer for up to 4 weeks.

BASIL

Basil leaves should be shredded, not chopped. Finely shredded basil may be frozen simply by placing it in a polythene bag; however beating it into butter gives a better result if you intend tossing freshly cooked pasta with the herb.

Preparation Carefully wash and dry the leaves, then shred them neatly using a pair of kitchen scissors. Mix the herb gently with softened butter.

Pack In a polythene bag or in a small rigid container. Alternatively, chill the butter, then cut it into small portions and open-freeze (page 93) them.

Storage Time The herb keeps well for up to 9 months; the butter for up to 3 months.

Use From frozen. Add shredded basil at the last minute to casseroles and sauces, toss it into cooked lentils, rice or pasta dishes. Melt the butter to go over hot pasta or fish. Use thawed pats of butter to top steaks, grilled chicken or fish steaks.

Pesto

This keeps perfectly well in the refrigerator for several months; however, if you are short of refrigerator space you may prefer to freeze some. Pound the leaves from a large bunch of basil to a paste with 2 garlic cloves and a handful of pine nuts. Save time by working them up in a food processor or blender. Add some freshly grated Parmesan cheese (about 25 g/1 oz to a large bunch of basil) and slowly pour in enough olive oil to make a soft, dark-green paste. Pack the pesto in a rigid container, then place it in a sealed polythene bag to freeze. It remains soft enough to spoon out as much as you need direct from the freezer.

BEANS, BROAD

These must be blanched, otherwise they do discolour (developing dark spots) and go rather bitter quite

quickly. Select young, tender beans for freezing.
Preparation Pod the beans, discarding any that are marked or very large.
Blanch For 2 minutes.
Storage Time Up to a year.
Use Put the frozen beans into boiling salted water and cook for about 5 minutes.

BEANS, FRENCH

These keep slightly better than broad beans without blanching but only for about a month. Pick tender young beans that are firm. On hot sunny days it is best to pick the beans in the morning as they tend to soften and become slightly limp in the sun.
Preparation Trim the ends off the beans, then wash and dry them. They may be cut into short lengths if preferred.
Blanch For 2 minutes.
Pack In usable quantities or open-freeze (page 93) in a single layer, then pack in a large bag.
Storage Time Up to 1 year.
Use Cook from frozen, in boiling salted water for about 5 minutes.

BEANS, RUNNER

These may be frozen without blanching for 4–6 weeks. Again, it is important to select tender young beans and to pick them early in the day so that they are firm.
Preparation String the beans, trim their ends and wash them well. Slice them lengthways or cut them into lengths as you prefer.
Blanch For 2 minutes.
Pack In usable quantities.
Use Cook from frozen in boiling salted water. Allow about 2–3 minutes once the water has returned to the boil for firm, tender slices.

BEEF
See meat (page 86).

BEETROOT
Select small whole beetroot rather than larger ones that may be slightly stringy in texture when thawed. When thawed, beetroot tends to be watery and is only suitable for serving cut up and dressed, or combined with other ingredients in baked dishes.

Preparation Cook the beetroot in its skin, in boiling salted water for about 45 minutes, or until tender. Drain and rub off the peel easily at once by holding the beetroot under cold water.

Pack Pack in polythene bags while hot, seal and place in a bowl of ice cubes and water to cool as rapidly as possible. Dry well, label and freeze.

Storage Time Up to 9 months.

Use Thaw the beetroot for several hours in the refrigerator. Slice and dress with oil and vineger, mayonnaise, soured cream or yogurt. Add seasoning and snipped chives or chopped spring onion. The thawed beetroot may also be used in baked dishes or to make soup.

BEURRE MANIE
A mixture of butter and flour in the proportion 40 g/1½ oz butter creamed with 25 g/1 oz plain flour. Small lumps are whisked into simmering liquid (sauces and stews) as thickening. Open-freeze (page 93) small dollops of similar known weight, then pack and freeze. Label with the quantity of flour and butter.

Storage Time Up to 3 months if made with salted butter, 6 months with unsalted.

BISCUITS
These can be frozen cooked in a rigid container but the best idea is to freeze the prepared mixture so that you

can bake a batch when needed.

Preparation   Shape the mixture in a roll, wrap and chill well before freezing. Alternatively, pipe the mixture on film-lined baking sheets and open-freeze (page 93).

Pack   In 2 pieces of cling film. Pack several rolls together in a polythene bag. Pack piped mixtures in a rigid container.

Storage Time   About 3–4 months.

Use   Bake from frozen, allowing an extra 5–10 minutes.

BLACKBERRIES

Both wild and cultivated freeze well. Select only large, juicy and ripe fruit.

Preparation   Wash and drain well.

Pack   In usable quantities with or without sugar or open-freeze (page 93).

Storage Time   Up to 1 year.

Use   From frozen; blackberries are best used in cooked dishes, such as fools, pies and crumbles, as they tend to be squashy when thawed.

BLACKCURRANTS

Really worth freezing because they have such a short season and are not readily available frozen commercially.

Preparation   Top and tail the fruit, then wash and dry it.

Pack   In usable quantities, with or without sugar added. The fruit may also be frozen in syrup (page 118).

Use   From frozen.

FREEZER TIP   Cook, purée, sieve and cool the fruit. Add sweetening to taste. Pack and label noting the quantity of sugar. Good for fools and sauces.

BLANCHING

Blanching is the term used for submerging food in boiling water (sometimes oil, but then known as 'blanching in oil') for a very short, exactly timed period.

Why Blanch? Fruit and vegetables naturally contain enzymes which promote ripening and subsequently deterioration in quality. They do not cause the food to go off but they act as a catalyst for the process. When food is frozen the action of enzymes is slowed down considerably but it is not stopped. The only way to stop the enzymes is by killing them and to do this, the food must he heated adequately.

To Blanch or Not to Blanch The rate at which vegetables deteriorate in flavour and texture if they are not blanched depends on their type; and individual taste plays a large part. Some people do not blanch vegetables at all and find them perfectly acceptable after many months in the freezer.

As a general rule, if you want to freeze a small quantity for a short period (about 2 weeks, or up to a month), there is no need to blanch. However, for longer storage always blanch first.

Technique It's important to get it right. The produce must not be cooked. Follow these rules:

1 Have a huge saucepan of rapidly boiling water ready. Have a large bowl full of iced water.
2 Use a wire basket to plunge batches of prepared produce into the water.
3 Bring the water back to the boil as rapidly as possible.
4 Time the blanching exactly from the moment the water comes back to a bubbling boil.
5 Lift the produce out of the water and plunge it straight into the iced water to prevent further cooking.
6 When cool, drain and dry on absorbent kitchen paper. Pack and seal at once.

FREEZER TIP   Only pick and prepare as much produce as you can blanch easily in one session.

Blanching in the Microwave
The microwave may be used for blanching small

quantities of produce. Following the manufacturer's instructions, cook the food for about a quarter of the recommended total cooking time. Plunge it straight into iced water.

Useful for small quantities of beans, peas, sweetcorn and apples. Not recommended for large amounts.

BOMBE
A bombe is a moulded, dome-shaped ice cream. Metal bombe moulds with lids are available from cookshops or a basin may be used instead. The ice cream (page 79) may be home-made or bought and you can combine two or three flavours. Soft-scoop ice creams are not suitable as they tend not to turn out well. Chill the mould. Spread a layer of ice cream inside it, over the bottom and evenly around the sides. Freeze. Add another layer. Freeze again. Finally fill the centre. Freeze until firm. Leave in the refrigerator for about 20 minutes before serving. Turn out the bombe and decorate with whipped cream and fruit.

BONES
When I bone out a chicken I always make stock from the bones; however, when time is short, I pack the carcass in a polythene bag and freeze it. Then I boil it up for stock later but always within about a month.

BOUQUETS GARNIS
Make up a selection of bouquets garnis from washed and dried sprigs of fresh garden herbs – try mint, rosemary and bay for lamb; sage, thyme and parsley for pork; bay, parsley, thyme or savory for beef; parsley, chives, bay and a strip of lemon peel for fish.
Pack Open-freeze (page 93), then pack and label with the content of each bouquet garni. Exclude the air in a polythene bag, then store in a rigid container to protect the bouquets garnis.

Storage Time   Up to 1 year.
Use   From frozen, as fresh.

BREAD

Freeze bread which is really fresh.
Preparation   Make sure the loaf has cooled after baking. Buying large loaves and cutting them in half is a great idea (my mother's) if there are just two of you.
Pack   In polythene bags, overwrapping the bought wrapper on sliced bread if you intend keeping it for more than 2 weeks.
Storage Time   Up to 3 months for large loaves. Up to 2 months for small loaves and rolls. French bread does not keep well for more than 2 weeks.
Use   Thaw large loaves in the refrigerator overnight or at room temperature for several hours. They may also be thawed in the oven set at a low to medium heat but they tend to be very crisp outside and dry out quickly when cooled. French bread and rolls may be heated through successfully from frozen.

Sliced bread may be used from frozen for toast and for making sandwiches to be eaten later in the same day.

Types of Bread

Uncooked Dough   Does not freeze successfully.
Bought Part-Baked Bread   Useful freezer stand-by. Buy it ready frozen and follow the manufacturer's instructions.

Speciality Breads   Worth freezing! As well as pitta (page 104), try storing nan, chapatis, Greek-style bread with seeds, Polish rye bread and dark pumpernickel.

BREADCRUMBS
Store fresh (white or brown) and dried breadcrumbs.
Pack   In polythene bags or a rigid container.
Storage Time   Up to 3 months for fresh crumbs; 6 months for dried crumbs
Use   From frozen for making small quantities of stuffing, for topping gratins, for coating food and so on.

BROCCOLI
Select tender broccoli spears, either calabrese or purple sprouting.
Preparation   Remove the excess, tough stalk. Wash well and dry.
Blanch   For 3 minutes.
Pack   In usable quantities in polythene bags or open-freeze (page 93) and pack in a large bag. Extract as much air as possible.
Storage Time   Up to 9 months.
Use   Straight from frozen. Cook in boiling water until tender, 5–10 minutes depending on the size and tenderness of the broccoli.

BRUSSELS SPROUTS
Select small, tight sprouts. It is important to blanch sprouts as they tend to develop a strong flavour even after a few days if frozen without blanching.
Preparation   Discard damaged and outer leaves. Cut a small cross into the base of each sprout – this ensures that the tougher stalk end cooks as quickly as the rest of the sprout. Thoroughly wash the sprouts.
Blanch   For 3 minutes.
Pack   Sprouts usually stay separate when frozen so it is easy to remove the required quantity.

Use Cook from frozen, adding to boiling water and simmering for about 5 minutes once the water has boiled again.

BUTTER
Only freeze butter which is absolutely fresh.
Pack Pack the butter in its wrapping in an outer freezer bag.
Storage Time Salted butter will keep for up to 3 months; unsalted for up to 6 months.
Use Thaw the butter overnight in the refrigerator or for about 3 hours in a cool room.

Flavoured Butters
These are a good freezer stand-by.
Herb Butter Beat chopped fresh herbs into butter. Mix parsley, chervil, tarragon, a little thyme, a little rosemary and a little mint, or make up other combinations as you wish.
Garlic Butter Not a good freezer candidate. Garlic tends to turn slightly 'tangy' if stored raw for a long time. Can be stored for a few weeks though.
Lemon Parsley Butter Beat grated lemon rind, chopped parsley and a little lemon juice into butter. Good with fish or chicken.
Pack Form into a roll, chill and slice. Pack in layers in a rigid container, separating the layers with cling film.
Storage Time Up to 3 months.
Use From frozen, removing as many slices as required.

BUTTERCREAM
Freeze any buttercream leftover from filling a cake.
Pack In a rigid container.
Storage time Up to 3 months.
Use Thaw in the refrigerator overnight, then beat well before using.

C

CABBAGE
I would not recommend freezing cabbage as my own attempts have been unsuccessful, both in taste and texture.

CAKES
See gâteaux (page 74).

All sorts of baked cakes freeze well.

Victoria Sandwich and Madeira-Type   Freeze without filling. Interleave layers with cling film.

Storage Time   Up to 3 months.

Small Cakes   Best cooked in paper cases. Pack in a rigid container. Store as for Victoria sandwich-type.

Storage Time   Up to 3 months.

Rubbed-in Cakes   For example, rock cakes. These freeze well. They should be closely wrapped in polythene as they tend to dry out quickly.

Storage Time   Up to 3 months.

Whisked Sponges   With little or no fat, these freeze very well. Best unfilled, layered with cling film. Protect in a rigid container.

Storage Time   Up to 6 months.

Swiss Rolls   Roll up in greaseproof paper, pack and store as for whisked sponges.

Storage Time   Up to 6 months.

Buttercream-decorated Cakes   As for gâteaux (page 74).

Storage Time   Up to 1 month.

Light Fruit Cakes   As for Victoria sandwich-type.

Storage Time   Up to 3 months.

Rich Fruit Cakes   No point in freezing these as they store well in a dry, cool place in an airtight container and their flavour matures.

Iced Cakes   Cakes decorated with glacé or royal icing do not freeze well. Those covered with sugarpaste may

be frozen; add decorations such as flowers on thawing.
Thawing Cakes   Plain cakes may be thawed at room temperature for a few hours or overnight. Whisked sponges thaw quickly; they may be layered with fillings and decorated while frozen. Creamed cakes take longer to thaw but they may be filled while frozen, then left to thaw. Add icing when thawed.

Small cakes thaw quickly and are ideal for packing in lunch boxes.

FREEZER TIP   Home-made cake makes wonderful trifle. Whisked sponges are best but creamed mixtures are far superior to bought alternatives.

Uncooked Cake Mixture
Whisked Sponge   Do not freeze: it collapses.
Creamed Mixture   This may be frozen in sandwich tins or in individual paper cake cases. Do not freeze in large, deep tins as the bulk is too much to thaw and cook successfully in one operation.
Preparation   Line the sandwich tins with cling film or freezer film, making sure it is smooth. Put the prepared mixture into the tins and spread it out evenly. Put paper cake cases in patty tins, divide the mixture between them. Freeze until hard.
Pack   Lift the mixture from the tins, remove the film and pack the block in a polythene bag. Separate two blocks with film.
Storage Time   Up to 2 months.
Use   Place in the greased tins and cook from frozen, allowing an extra 7–10 minutes. Allow an extra 5–7 minutes for small cakes.

CARROTS
Large, old carrots are not worth freezing but small new whole ones or cut-up medium ones are a good stand-by.
Preparation   Trim and scrub small whole carrots. Trim, scrub or peel and dice medium carrots. Time

permitting, cut in julienne strips instead of dice.

Blanch   For 2–3 minutes, the shorter time for diced or julienne carrots.

Pack   In usable portions in bags, excluding all air. Julienne strips and dice may be packed in boilable bags ready for heating from frozen for crunchy results.

Storage Time   Up to 1 year.

Use   Cook from frozen, allowing 5–10 minutes in boiling salted water or until the vegetables are cooked to taste. Small quantities of julienne strips may simply be cooked with a spoonful of water and knob of butter until thawed and the liquor reduced to a glaze.

CASSEROLES AND STEWS

Meat, poultry and game casseroles and stews freeze well. Vegetable and bean casseroles freeze reasonably well provided that they are slightly undercooked before freezing. Fish casseroles do not freeze well – the cooked fish becomes very dry and tasteless.

Preparation   When making casseroles for freezing there are a few points to remember for best results.

* Trim meat of excess fat before cooking.
* Poultry is best skinned.
* Make sure tough cuts are cooked until thoroughly tender.
* Add root vegetables right at the end of cooking, so that they are 'blanched' but not tender. Or add them to the thawed casserole before reheating.
* Mushrooms should be added after thawing.
* Keep salt and pepper seasoning to the minimum. Moderate the use of strongly flavoured herbs as they can become more pronounced during longer storage.
* Remove herb sprigs, bouquets garnis, bay leaves and whole spices from the cooled casserole before freezing.
* Cool the casserole as quickly as possible and skim off all fat before freezing.

* Make sure there is enough sauce or liquor to keep the ingredients moist.
* Add thickenings such as beurre manié (page 40) or cornflour blended with water when reheating.
* **Do not** add cream or eggs to casseroles to enrich or thicken them before freezing as they curdle. Add after reheating.

Packing Always pack casseroles in quantities to suit your needs.

Rigid Containers – select a size that allows a little headspace (page 77) but which is small enough to keep the ingredients in their sauce. Do not store small amounts in large containers as they develop ice crystals on the surface and any meat or poultry which is above the sauce tends to develop freezer burn (page 69).

Polythene Bags – use strong ones. For small portions, simply make sure the bags are well supported until the contents are frozen – place them on a baking sheet or in a container to avoid any danger of the bag puncturing. For larger quantities, line a freezer-proof basin or other container with the bag, then fill, seal and label. Freeze until hard, then remove the container and store the package. Blocks prepared this way are neat for storage.

Boilable Bags – for reheating casseroles and stews from frozen. Ideal for small amounts and for microwave use when sealed with microwave-proof ties. Follow guidance for polythene bags.

Blocks of Stew – to reheat a stew in the original dish in which it was cooked, turn it out to cool in a clean, covered bowl. Wash the cooking dish well, line it with foil (as uncreased as possible), then return the stew to it. Freeze until hard, remove the block of stew and pack. The unwrapped block may be returned to the cooking dish for thawing and reheating. On the label make a note of any other ingredients that are to be added – thickening, seasoning or vegetables.

Storage Time   From 3 to 6 months, depending on the ingredients and personal preference. Store the food only for as long as the shortest period recommended for individual ingredients. Plain beef or chicken casseroles, with the minimum of fat, plenty of liquid and no strong seasonings freeze well for over 6 months, up to 9–12 months.

Fatty meats and ingredients such as bacon reduce the freezer life of the dish. If the dish is well salted it will not keep as long, as salt tends to promote rancidity in fats.

Provided that the food is properly prepared and packed for freezing, the acceptable storage life depends on individual taste. For example, some people may find that onions, garlic, herbs and spices become too developed in flavour after a short period; others may not notice the difference after several months.

Use   Either thaw the dish slowly overnight in the refrigerator or by reheating it very slowly in the oven, on the hob or following the manufacturer's instructions in a microwave. Boil-in-the-bag packs may be reheated from frozen: they must be thoroughly hot before being served.

The vital point to remember is that the food must be thoroughly thawed and reheated properly to the original temperature at which it was cooked before being eaten. This ensures that any bacteria that developed between cooling and freezing, or thawing and heating, are destroyed.

Always break up and stir stews during reheating. Make sure they are thoroughly heated before adding any thickening ingredients. Vegetables that are to be cooked in the stew should be added once it is thawed and two-thirds heated. Root vegetables are best par-cooked before adding so that they are tender when the stew is thoroughly hot.

Thawing in the refrigerator overnight is best and reheating on Medium in the microwave is very successful.

CAULIFLOWER

It is important that cauliflower is absolutely fresh, crisp and white. Blanching is important to preserve quality.

Preparation Trim off the leaves and tough stalks. Break into small florets of equal size. Wash and drain.

Blanch For 3 minutes.

Storage Time About 9–12 months.

Use From frozen. Cook in boiling salted water for about 5–7 minutes. Drain well.

FREEZER TIP Cauliflower cheese freezes very well. Best prepared in individual portions so that it may be baked from frozen. Make sure the vegetable is drained thoroughly before coating in the sauce.

CELERIAC

Do not freeze raw; this is best cooked and mashed.

Preparation Peel, rinse well and cook in boiling salted water until tender. Mash with butter, pepper and a little milk. Cover and cool.

Pack In a rigid container or bag. Label with a note as to the seasoning, butter and milk added.

Storage Time Up to 3 months.

Use Thaw overnight in the refrigerator or for several hours at room temperature. Beat well. Reheat, covered, in the oven or a steamer; or top with breadcrumbs and cheese, then bake until hot and golden.

CELERY

Although sliced celery may be frozen as part of a cooked dish, this vegetable does not freeze successfully. However, celery soup freezes well for 3–4 months.

CHEESE

See fromage frais (page 70)

Blocks of Hard Cheese, such as Cheddar, do not have as good a texture on thawing, since they tend to be slightly crumbly. Leftovers from a cheeseboard can be frozen. With careful thawing, the cheese usually tastes fine for a quick supper, with plenty of warm crusty bread.

Grated Hard Cheese, such as Cheddar, freezes very well and may be used from frozen for adding to sauces, sprinkling on toast for grilling and so on.

Cottage Cheese The curds in cottage cheese tend to become grainy and small.

Mozzarella freezes well for use in cooking. Either pack in a piece, then part-thaw it until you can slice it for use or slice the cheese first, open-freeze (page 93) it, then pack it. Good for topping pizza and baked vegetable dishes.

Parmesan Frozen grated Parmesan cheese is a real boon. Buy some good-quality freshly grated cheese from an Italian delicatessen, freeze it and use as required without thawing.

Soft Cheese Curd cheese, quark and cream cheeses freeze well. Thaw them in the refrigerator overnight and stir well before using.

Storage Time 4–6 months.

CHEESECAKE

Baked cheesecakes and the heavier chilled cheesecakes with gelatine freeze reasonably well. However, light cheesecakes which rely solely on gelatine for a 'set' and to retain shape do not freeze well.

Preparation Thaw whole or cut into portions. Add any piped cream or fruit topping after the cheesecake is thawed.

Pack Wrap individual portions in cling film, then place in a polythene bag. Pack a whole cheesecake in a rigid container.

Storage Time Up to 3 months.

Use Thaw overnight or for several hours in the refrigerator. Stand slices on absorbent kitchen paper on a plate to mop up any drips.

CHERRIES
These are really worth freezing, either in syrup, with or without sugar.

Preparation Wash and dry the cherries, then stone them, catching all the juices that drip out. Mix the cherries and their juice with some sugar, if liked, or submerge the fruit in syrup (page 118).

Pack In usable amounts in polythene bags or in rigid containers with syrup. Alternatively, open-freeze (page 93).

Use Use from frozen. Unsweetened cherries may be used for savoury cooking as well as in sweet dishes.

CHESTNUTS
Cooked and left whole or puréed, these are terrific freezer fare.

Preparation Wash the chestnuts, then make a split in each one. Boil for about 10 minutes or until just tender. Peel the chestnuts and cover until cooled. They may be puréed in a blender or food processor, or by rubbing them through a sieve.

Pack In polythene bags, excluding as much air as possible. Pack the purée in a rigid container, allowing a little headspace (page 77). Whole chestnuts may be frozen in a container of heavy syrup (page 118) for use in desserts later.

Storage Time Up to 1 year.

Use Thaw for several hours at room temperature or leave the purée overnight in the refrigerator. The purée may be sweetened and used to make a variety of desserts. Unsweetened purée is useful for stuffings. Cooked chestnuts are also used in stuffings, in pies or other savoury cooking.

CHICKEN
Good-quality commercially frozen whole birds are a better option than home-frozen chickens because they

are frozen more rapidly. However, there is no reason why you should not freeze raw chicken. Remember to turn the freezer to the fast-freeze setting well in advance, following the manufacturer's instructions.

Only freeze absolutely fresh chicken which has not previously been frozen. **Do not** stuff the body cavity before freezing a chicken. Whole or jointed birds may be frozen.

Preparation Trim unwanted joint ends and remove the giblets from whole birds. Rinse the body cavity of whole chickens under cold running water, drain well and dry on absorbent kitchen paper. Trim off any obvious pieces of fat and unwanted flaps of skin. Truss the bird into a neat shape.

Pack Cover any bone ends or sharp pieces of protruding bone which may pierce the bag, with small pads of foil. Exclude air from the bag and seal.

Joints and boneless breasts should be wrapped in cling film or packed in numbers intended for future use.

Storage Time 9–12 months. Check the storage time for commercially frozen chicken on the wrapping.

Use Thaw chicken thoroughly in the refrigerator before use. Leave the chicken in its wrapping, place it in a large dish near the bottom of the refrigerator and be sure it does not drip. A small-to-medium whole chicken will need to thaw between 12 and 24 hours in the refrigerator. Joints should be left overnight. Large chickens take 1–2 days to thaw.

Rinse the thawed bird under cold water. Pat it dry and make sure it is completely thawed before cooking. Remember to check that it is cooked through before serving!

Cooked Chicken

Any leftover cooked chicken should be cooled rapidly, chilled, then frozen promptly. To prevent it drying out, carve the chicken into slices or cut it into chunks, then cover with gravy or a sauce such as mushroom or parsley sauce.

Use Thaw completely in the refrigerator, preferably overnight. Reheat thoroughly until the sauce is boiling and the chicken hot through.

CHILLIES

Fresh green or red chillies freeze well.

Preparation Cut off the stalks, remove the seeds, rinse, dry and chop.

Pack Wrap 1–2 chopped chillies in small pieces of cling film, screwing them up tightly. Pack them in a polythene bag and note the number of chillies in each little pack on the label.

Storage Time Up to 9 months.

Use From frozen as fresh.

CHILLING FOOD

Food should be as cold as possible when it is placed in the freezer. Ideally, chill in the refrigerator first. This is particularly important when freezing cooked dishes.

The freezer is also useful for chilling food quickly. For example, chill puff pastry quickly between stages of rolling in the butter. However, never put hot food in the freezer as it will raise the temperature of the frozen foods.

CHOCOLATE

There is not much point in freezing chocolate as it keeps well in the refrigerator for long periods. Chocolate shapes and other decorations develop 'bloom' – a whitening on the surface, harmless but unattractive - if frozen.

Chocolate Caraque

Make a large batch and freeze some in a rigid container for use as instant decoration on desserts and gâteaux.

Pour melted chocolate on a marble slab or foil. When set, use a long-bladed kitchen knife to shave off long curls. Open-freeze (page 93), then pack in layers in a rigid container with interleaving film between each delicate layer. Make white chocolate caraque too – it looks very impressive mixed with dark caraque and the combination cleverly disguises 'bloom'!

CHOUX PASTRY

Uncooked choux pastry freezes well and it cooks quickly from frozen to give excellent results. Freshly cooked pastries have a slightly better texture than those that have been frozen, thawed and crisped (these tend to be slightly dry).

Preparation, uncooked   Pipe buns, éclairs or a ring on a film-lined tray. Alternatively, pipe a gougère edge around the inside of a lined baking dish.

Preparation, cooked   Make and bake buns, éclairs or choux ring. Split as soon as they are removed from the oven, then cool on a wire rack. Bake a gougère edge, without filling, in a foil-lined dish. Cool, remove from dish.

Pack   Pack small cooked items in a rigid container. Wrap large rings or gougère edges in foil or film, then in a polythene bag, excluding as much air as possible. However, if using a vacuum pump take care not to draw out too much air, making the choux collapse. Uncooked items may be open-frozen (page 93), then packed in a polythene bag.

Storage Time   Up to 6 months.

Use, raw   Place the required number of items on a greased baking sheet and cook from frozen, allowing an extra 3–5 minutes at the end of the cooking time for buns and éclairs or other small items; 7–10 minutes for a large ring or gougère.

Use, cooked   Thaw at room temperature for 2–3 hours. Crisp cooked choux items in the oven at 220°C/

425°F/gas 7 for 2–3 minutes. Cool, then fill and serve soon, before the pastry loses its crisp texture.

COCONUT
Fresh coconut may be frozen for short periods.
Preparation   Depends on what you intend doing with the coconut. Once shelled, it may be coarsely grated ready for use in desserts or to serve with suitable savoury dishes. Alternatively, soak the coconut in boiling water, then cool and strain it to make coconut milk.

Toasted coarsely grated fresh coconut may also be frozen for decorating gâteaux or desserts.
Pack   In rigid containers if toasted, otherwise in polythene bags. Pack coconut milk in rigid containers with headspace (page 77).
Storage Time   Up to 2 months. Remember that coconut has a high fat content, therefore, it will not keep for long periods without beginning to go rancid.
Use   Thaw as much grated as required. Thaw coconut milk in the refrigerator overnight or at room temperature for a few hours. Use as fresh.
FREEZER TIP   Freeze coconut milk in ice-cube trays, then pack in polythene bags - ideal for adding to spicy dishes.

COD
See fish (page 67).

COFFEE
Freeze roasted coffee beans or ground coffee to keep it really fresh.
Pack   Do not freeze tins or jars but leave foil packs unopened. Pack in polythene bags: use two if the coffee is loose to prevent it imparting its flavour to other foods. Label with the type.
Storage Time   Up to 1 year.
Use   From frozen as fresh.

FREEZER TIP If you make strong coffee (particularly espresso), freeze any freshly cooled excess in ice-cube trays. Pack in bags to use as a flavouring or for making milk shakes.

COMPLETE MEALS
The best way to freeze complete meals is to make dishes such as cottage pie, cobbler (stew with savoury scones on top), lasagne, stuffed pancakes or pizza, which are all satisfying enough to form a main meal, perhaps with a simple salad accompaniment. These should all be thawed and reheated thoroughly before serving.
FREEZER TIP Freeze individual portions of ready-made dishes in boilable bags. Reheat in a saucepan of boiling water or in the microwave until thoroughly hot. Rice (page 110) may also be prepared in this way.

COOKING FROM FROZEN
Only do this when recommended, for example, for fruit and vegetables, commercial products (follow the manufacturer's instructions carefully) and certain prepared foods.

Always thaw chicken and meat before cooking. If you are cooking prepared items from frozen, always ensure that the food is thoroughly heated or cooked through.
Why Take Care? Food and prepared dishes contain bacteria; some will be there naturally, others will be contracted from the air and surroundings. This is not hazardous unless the bacteria are allowed to multiply or unless certain foods are not cooked, in which case some harmful bacteria are not killed. See packing food (page 94) for notes on handling frozen food.

For example, chicken must always be cooked through because it may contain salmonella bacteria which cause food poisoning. If it is cooked directly from frozen, then there is greater risk that the meat will be raw in the centre or near the bone.

In the case of cooked dishes, food that is cooling and chilling provides the ideal warm environment for bacteria to multiply. The same is true when the food is thawing and gradually warming. Therefore, cooked foods must be thoroughly reheated to a temperature which will kill off any bacteria. The correct handling of food to be eaten cold is all important.

Quality In the majority of cases, the reason for thawing foods before cooking is because of quality. If some food is cooked from frozen (for example joints of meat), the outside may well be overcooked by the time the middle is just cooked.

CORN-ON-THE-COB

A good pick-your-own crop – select tender young cobs for freezing.

Preparation Remove the outer husk and silk. Trim the ends, wash and dry.

Blanch For 3–5 minutes.

Pack Wrap in cling film and pack in polythene bags.

Storage Time Up to 1 year.

Use Cook from frozen in boiling salted water for about 15 minutes.

FREEZER TIP Sweetcorn that has been frozen for too long tends to be tough and starchy. Cook it in boiling water, then scrape off all the kernels and use to make soup.

COURGETTES

I would not recommend freezing courgettes as they are far too soggy when thawed. It is better to cook them in a chunky ratatouille.

CRAB

Place a live crab in a carrier bag in the freezer to kill it before cooking. This is considered to be one of the more humane methods. Leave it for 8–12 hours to be sure that it is dead before cooking, allowing a little longer than normal.

Cooked crab meat may be frozen for up to 3 months. Keep the brown and white meat separate. Use for cooked dishes, gratins, pâtés and so on rather than for serving plain.

CRANBERRIES
The short season when they are available fresh makes these a freezer 'must' for anyone who appreciates their tangy flavour.
Preparation Wash and dry well.
Pack In polythene bags or rigid containers.
Storage Time Up to 1 year.
Use From frozen.

CREAM
Ready-frozen sticks or chips of single, whipping or double cream are easy to use in small quantities at a time; ideal for adding to sauces. For pouring or whipping, always thaw well before use, preferably in the refrigerator, following the packet instructions. Overheating in an attempt at rapid thawing causes the cream to separate.
Whipped Cream Double or whipping cream may be home-frozen if whipped first.
Pack Pack in rigid containers ready for folding into mixtures or serving with desserts.
Storage Time Up to 6 months.
Use Thaw slowly in the refrigerator for several hours or overnight.
FREEZER TIP Pipe rosettes or large swirls of whipped double cream on film-lined trays and open-freeze (page 93). Pack in rigid containers. Use straight from frozen, to decorate gâteaux or desserts. Allow to thaw for about 30 minutes at room temperature or up to 2 hours in the refrigerator.

CROISSANTS

Buy ready-frozen and store according to packet instructions. Or freeze good-quality freshly baked ones for up to 2 months. Pack in rigid containers to prevent crushing. Thaw for 2 hours at room temperature, then heat under a moderate grill or in the oven.

Home-made Croissants

These really are worth it! If you have the urge to do some baking, make a batch of croissants and freeze them. Alternatively, they may be frozen for up to 2 months when risen and ready to bake. Bake from frozen, allowing up to an extra 5 minutes on the recommended recipe time. The batch I tested only took about 3 minutes extra from frozen, but this will vary. Wonderful! Good made with equal quantities of wholemeal and strong white flour.

CRUMBLE MIXTURE

Freeze ready-mixed sweet or savoury crumble mixture. Rub margarine or butter into plain flour in the proportions half fat to flour.
Pack   In a polythene bag.
Use   Remove as much as required. Ground almonds, chopped nuts or grated orange rind may be added to the sweet crumble. Herbs, finely chopped onion and seasoning may be added to the savoury mixture. Sprinkle over the chosen base and cook from frozen, allowing an extra 5–10 minutes, depending on thickness and quantity of crumble.

CRUMPETS

These freeze well for up to 3 months.
Pack   In a heavy freezer bag.
Use   Toast from frozen.

CUCUMBER
Do not freeze cucumber – it becomes soggy and unacceptable.

CUSTARD
No custard made with eggs should be frozen. The eggs curdle leaving the mixture separated on thawing.

Pouring custard made with custard powder may be frozen in the same way as sauces thickened with cornflour. On thawing the custard will be slightly thinned and it will need thoroughly whisking before being reheated.

D

DAMSONS
Freeze as for plums (page 104).

DRIP OR FREEZER DRIP
This is the term used for the liquid which seeps out of some frozen foods as they thaw. The liquid from fish, poultry, meat and game should be discarded. Liquid from frozen fruit should be saved as it contains a good deal of flavour and juice. Moisture from foods such as cheese should be mopped up on absorbent kitchen paper as the food thaws.

DRY-PACK
A term sometimes used when freezing fruit, usually meaning the same as open-freeze (page 93). May sometimes be used in the context of packing fruit plain, without any added sugar or syrup. Dry-sugar-pack is fruit which is sprinkled or coated with sugar and packed.

DUCK

Good-quality commercially frozen duck, whole or in portions, is readily available. However, fresh duck may be frozen.

Preparation Trim off any lumps of fat, rinse the bird in cold water and dry it thoroughly with absorbent kitchen paper.

Pack In a polythene bag, extracting as much air as possible.

Storage Time 4–6 months, depending on the fat content – the fatter the bird, the shorter the storage life.

Use Thaw duck in the refrigerator; overnight for a whole bird, 4–6 hours for portions.

FREEZER TIP Look out for frozen packs of Peking duck (produced by Cherry Valley) in supermarkets and freezer centres – the duck, sauces and pancakes are of excellent quality.

DUMPLINGS

Cooked suet dumplings freeze well. Pack them separately from a casserole. Thaw at room temperature for 1–2 hours, then reheat on top of a casserole in the oven or on the hob.

E

EGGS

These may be frozen as a stand-by or if you have a few too many home laid eggs. Also, yolks or whites left after making mayonnaise or icing may be frozen. Without added salt or sugar, yolks thicken on freezing. Only freeze very fresh eggs. Do not freeze whole eggs in their shells. Do not freeze cooked eggs or dishes which contain cooked eggs (for example, fish pie with hard-boiled eggs or Scotch eggs).

Preparation   Beat whole eggs. Add ½ teaspoon salt or 2 teaspoons sugar to every 4 eggs. Lightly beat yolks with 1 teaspoon salt or 2 tablespoons sugar to every 4 yolks. Whites may be frozen without whisking and without salt or sugar.

Pack   In small rigid containers, allowing a little headspace (page 77). Place in a polythene bag or seal with freezer tape. Note the number of whites and the quantity of salt or sugar to the number of eggs or yolks on the label.

Storage Time   Whole eggs may be stored for 6–9 months. Whites for 9–12 months. Yolks for 4–6 months.

Use   Thaw the eggs in the refrigerator for about 4–6 hours. Alternatively, leave them in a cool room for 2–3 hours. Lightly beat the eggs before use.

FREEZER TIP   If you forget to label the container, here is a rough guide to the volume of lightly beaten, or whisked, egg.

1 size 3 egg, beaten = about 4 tablespoons
1 yolk = 1 tablespoon
1 white = 2 tablespoons.

ENZYMES

Enzymes are proteins that act as catalysts in the on-going chemical reactions that are part of life. They are present in all living organisms but for freezing purposes it is the enzymes in vegetables that are highlighted.

Enzymes promote the deterioration in quality of food, just as they promote all other organic reactions. When food is frozen the action of enzymes is slowed down considerably; however, it is not stopped completely as the enzymes themselves are not destroyed. This means that over long periods of freezer storage, some deterioration in quality will be caused unless the enzymes are destroyed by heating. Temperatures of between 77–100°C/170–212°F are required. It is also worth remembering that in very warm conditions, or under the influence of gentle heat, enzymes become more effective. For this reason, vegetables are blanched (page 41) before freezing: they are plunged into rapidly boiling water so that the enzymes are destroyed as quickly as possible. The vegetables are blanched in small batches so that they are heated very quickly.

F

FAST-FREEZE
See temperature guide (page 120).

FAT
Fat turns rancid mainly because of oxidation. Saturated fats are composed of molecules that have a 'neat' structure. Unsaturated fats have a structure with atoms that are available for bonding on to others from outside. Oxygen atoms attach themselves to these free atoms in a process known as oxidation. This causes the fat to develop an unpleasant flavour.

Animal foods are made up of both saturated as well as unsaturated fats and the unsaturated ones oxidize more readily.

Pork, chicken and fatty fish such as mackerel contain more unsaturated fat than beef, and their fat goes rancid more quickly. The salt content of the food also affects the rate at which the fat turns rancid. Salted butter and cured bacon will become rancid more quickly than unsalted butter or pork.

FATLESS SPONGES
See cakes (page 47).

FENNEL
See herbs (page 77).

Florence fennel is the bulbous vegetable which has an aniseed-like flavour and a texture similar to that of celery. The vegetable does not freeze well, becoming limp on thawing. Finely diced fennel, incorporated in cooked dishes, may be frozen.

FILO PASTRY
Available from supermarkets, delicatessens and freezer centres. Store for the time recommended on the packet. Once thawed the whole packet of pastry leaves has to be used – if it is re-frozen, the pastry tends to become brittle or the leaves stick together.

Leftover pastry may be filled and shaped into small triangular pasties, then frozen to be cooked at a later date. Store the shaped pastries for 2–3 months, then cook them from frozen, allowing an extra 5-10 minutes baking.

FISH
See also crab (page 60), lobster (page 83), mussels (page 91), prawns (page 106), salmon (page 112) and smoked fish (page 114).

Fish freezes well raw. Only the freshest fish should be frozen. Purchased frozen fish is of a very high quality and it is processed rapidly after catching. If you buy from a fishmonger, make sure that the fish has not been frozen and thawed for sale. (See prawns, page 106.) Buying quantities of fish from a fishmonger for long-term storage is not recommended – it is fine for a few days but if you intend keeping the fish for 3–6 months, then it should be freshly caught. Always follow storage and cooking instructions on packs of any frozen fish products.

Preparation Whole fish should be gutted, rinsed and dried. De-scale and trim the fish. Skin fillets, if wished, and trim steaks or cutlets. Boning cutlets or fillets before freezing also saves time later.

Packing Wrap portions of fish individually in cling film. Then pack them together in a polythene bag. To keep the body cavity of large fish in shape, place some crumpled cling film or foil in it.

Storage Time White fish may be frozen for 3–4 months. Oily fish may be frozen for 2–3 months but these **must** be frozen freshly caught.

Use If grilling or frying, thaw the fish in the refrigerator, then pat it dry and use as required. Fish which is to be cooked gently by a moist method may be cooked from frozen.

FREEZER TIP   It is important to exclude as much air as possible from packs of oily fish. One way of doing this is to coat the whole fish in ice. Open-freeze (page 93) the fish. Have a bowl of water well chilled in the freezer. Dip the fish in the water, then replace it on a lined tray and freeze. Repeat several times until the fish is thoroughly coated in a layer of ice. Pack.

Cooked Fish

This does not freeze well as the flakes become very dry. Cooked fish in a thickened sauce (for example in fish pie) is acceptable, also in fish cakes or fish croquettes.

FLANS

See quiche (page 106).

Filled and unfilled flans may be frozen. The recommended storage time for all the following is up to 3 months.

Pastry Flan Cases Unfilled pastry cases may be frozen either raw, part-cooked or cooked. Freeze them in flan tins, suitable dishes or foil cases. Thaw in the refrigerator for a few hours. Cooked pastry cases should be crisped by placing in a heated oven or under a moderate grill for a few minutes.

Sweet pastry may be enriched by adding chopped nuts or ground almonds and grated orange rind. Once crisped the flan case may be filled with crème pâtissière or custard, then topped with fresh or canned fruit.

Savoury Filled Flans Pastry flans filled with a sauce mixture freeze well ready to cook from frozen. Salmon, tuna, diced cooked chicken or diced cooked ham may be mixed in a Béchamel sauce with cooked onions and cheese. A breadcrumb topping may be added.

Sponge Flans Follow storage times as for cakes (page 47). Make either fatless sponge or a creamed mixture. Pack and freeze empty. The flans may be filled when frozen, then allowed to thaw or they may be thawed before filling.

Crumb Cases Crushed biscuits combined with butter and used to line a flan dish may also be frozen for short periods but this type of case is very fragile.

FRANKFURTERS

Vacuum packs of frankfurters may be frozen for about 2 months. They are best used in cooked dishes when thawed rather than eaten cold.

FREEZER BURN

This is the term used for a dried-out surface on food, caused by inadequate packing. The surface of meat or fish will look pale and dry; vegetables, for example French beans, will be lightly spotted with grey or whitish patches. The affected area is not dangerous to eat but it lacks flavour and poultry or meat will be toughened. Always check packs of meat and fish in less-busy shops to make sure they are not damaged by freezer burn.

FROMAGE FRAIS
Both plain and flavoured type freeze well. Frozen samples of virtually fat-free and 8% fat fromage frais thawed successfully without curdling. At first the fromage frais looked as though it had separated, but a good stir restored its original texture. Cartons of sweetened fruit fromage frais should be stirred before eating. I have not tested long-term storage, but would suggest a time of about 2 months.

FROZEN FOODS, COMMERCIAL
For safe shopping, storage and use follow these guidelines.

☆ Take frozen foods from the freezer last as you go around a supermarket.
☆ Carry frozen foods in a chiller bag.
☆ Take them home promptly and put them straight in the freezer.
☆ Follow the manufacturer's recommended storage life.
☆ Follow the manufacturer's thawing and cooking or reheating instructions.
☆ Make sure that food which is reheated is thoroughly hot before serving.

FRUIT
See apples (page 30), bananas (page 37), cherries (page 54) and so on.

Fruit for freezing should be perfect and absolutely

fresh. Pick-your-own farms are the ideal place to buy fruit but don't be tempted to pick far more than you can process easily.

Exotic Fruit

Unfortunately, many of the exotic fruits do not freeze well but often they may be used to make excellent sorbets and ice creams. Remember that crisp-textured, juicy fruit will probably break down to a limp texture on thawing. Full-flavoured fruits may be puréed and frozen.

Carambola   Also known as star fruit. This does not freeze well as its crisp texture becomes limp and the skin toughens.

Kiwi Fruits   Do not freeze well but their purée may be used to make exciting sorbets (page 115).

Kumquats   These may be frozen uncooked or poached in syrup (page 118). Wash and dry well before freezing raw.

Lychee   The stoned flesh may be frozen in light or medium syrup (page 118).

Mango   Whole mangoes do not freeze well. The sliced fruit may be frozen in syrup (page 118). Mango purée, mixed with a little lemon juice and sweetened if liked,

freezes well for use in sauces, mousses and other desserts.

Passion Fruit   Freeze whole or scoop the fruit out of the shells, then place it in small containers. Alternatively, use the juice to flavour ice cream (page 79), or sorbet (page 115).

Paw Paw   The sliced fruit (or chunks) may be frozen in syrup. Paw paw purée, mixed with a little lemon juice and sweetened if liked, also freezes well. Good for making ice cream (page 79).

Prickly Pear   This does not freeze well. The seed-studded flesh is crisp and refreshing, with a delicate flavour. On freezing the texture becomes limp and the flavour is too delicate for making sorbets or ice cream.

FRUIT CAKE
See cakes (page 47).

G

GAME
Because of the limited seasons, game is an ideal freezer candidate.

Game Birds
In general, game birds – for example, pheasant, partridge, grouse and wild duck – should be treated as for chicken. Before freezing, game should be prepared as for cooking; it should be hung, plucked, drawn, cleaned, jointed or trussed as required.

Game must be hung before freezing so that it develops flavour and becomes tender. After thawing, it should be treated as for poultry and used promptly. Game which is to be frozen for longer than 2 weeks should be hung for slightly less time than normally required.

Storage Time Wild duck should be used within 6 months (because of the fat content). Other game birds may be stored for up to 9 months, as long as they are not very well hung before freezing.

Venison

Venison is a lean meat which freezes well. Farmed venison is available throughout the year. A whole carcass should be prepared by a butcher, hung and jointed.

Venison should be trimmed of all fat before cooking as the fat has a rather unpleasant taste. Joints may be larded with pork fat and trussed before freezing but this does reduce the storage life to 3–4 months. Alternatively, joints may be trussed before freezing, then barded with fat on thawing.

Wrap steaks individually, then place them in a polythene bag for storage. Cubes of venison for braising or stewing may be open-frozen (page 93) or packed in usable portions. Minced venison should be packed in portions ready for use. Venison sausages also freeze successfully.

Storage Time Venison keeps well for 9–12 months.
FREEZER TIP Label game with a note on the best cooking method – for example, note whether a pheasant is a hen (tender, for roasting) or cock (for stewing).

GARLIC
See butter (page 46).

I have never had problems when freezing dishes that are flavoured with garlic (with the significant exception of butter) and stored for about 3–4 months.
FREEZER TIP Think about the overall flavour of the dish before freezing: for example, if the garlic is well balanced by other full-flavoured ingredients, then it is unlikely to dominate the dish when thawed.

GARLIC BREAD

Freezes very well. Beat some butter (page 46) with crushed garlic, then spread it on slices of French bread and re-shape the loaf. Pack in foil, then place in a polythene bag. Pack two or more short loaves together in one bag.

Storage Time   About 1–2 months.

Use   Bake from frozen, in the foil wrapping, allowing about 20 minutes at 200°C/400°F/gas 6.

GATEAUX

Decorated gâteaux may be frozen for short periods, either filled with fresh cream or buttercream (page 46) and decorated. Do not add any fruit decoration or similar topping which will either lose its good texture or drip on thawing. Do not add any glaze or jellied filling or topping.

Open-freeze (page 93) the decorated gâteau, then place it in a large rigid container with an airtight lid. In a well-sealed container a gâteau will usually keep for up to a month. Alternatively, wrap the gâteau in a double-thick tent of heavy-duty foil and store it with great care. In this case it should not be frozen for longer than 2 weeks. Thaw in its covered container in the refrigerator overnight.

GELATINE

Dishes stiffened with gelatine do not retain a good set. The ice crystals which form in the food break down the cells to some extent. Although it is possible to freeze mousse set with gelatine in the serving dish, the texture is not as good as it ought to be when thawed.

GENOESE SPONGE

See cakes (page 47).

GOAT'S MILK

This may be purchased ready-frozen or it can be home-frozen. Pour it into a rigid container and leave headspace (page 77). Cover and freeze.

Storage Time 1–2 months, or as recommended when purchased.

Use Thaw overnight, or for several hours, in the refrigerator.

GOOSE

Since it has a high fat content, goose has a shorter freezer life than other poultry.

Preparation The bird should be cleaned, trimmed and trussed ready for cooking. Be sure to cut away any lumps of fat.

Pack In a polythene bag, extracting as much air as possible. Make sure the bone ends do not pierce the bag – pad them with pieces of foil or cling film first if necessary.

Storage Time Up to 4 months.

Use Make sure the bird is thoroughly thawed before cooking. Place it in the refrigerator for 24 hours or longer. See thawing (page 121).

GOOSEBERRIES

These freeze very well, either raw or cooked to a purée.

Preparation Top and tail the fruit, then wash and thoroughly dry it.

Pack With or without sugar in polythene bags. The fruit rarely freezes in a lump so it is automatically free-flow for use from frozen.

Storage Time A good year!

Use Use from frozen.

FREEZER TIP Frozen sweetened gooseberry purée is a great stand-by for making a quick fruit fool. Thaw in a saucepan over a low heat until two-thirds thawed, then whip in a food processor or blender until smooth. Mix with cold custard (canned in an emergency!), whipped cream or fromage frais and serve.

GRANITA
A form of water ice or sorbet (page 115) which is allowed to develop ice crystals to give it a crunchy texture. Unlike sorbet, granita is whisked only once, very briefly, during freezing.

GRAPEFRUIT JUICE
Freshly squeezed grapefruit juice is worth freezing.
Pack   In usable quantities in rigid containers leaving headspace (page 77).
Storage Time   Up to 1 year.
Use   Thaw in the refrigerator overnight or for a few hours, depending on quantity.

GRAPES
Not worth freezing for eating. However, they may be frozen for making wine at a later date, in which case the fruit should be prepared ready for pulping and fermenting. Alternatively, the grapes may be taken off their stalks and pulped, then frozen.

GRAVY
Freeze any leftover gravy made after roasting a joint. Label it with the type of meat – pork, lamb, beef, chicken and so on. It will keep for about 3–4 months.

H

HADDOCK
See fish (page 67) and smoked fish (page 114).

HAM, COOKED
Cooked ham may be frozen for short periods but only for use in cooked dishes when thawed. On thawing it has a slightly watery texture that makes it unsuitable for

serving on its own. Cooking a joint of ham on the bone is a comparatively economical way of feeding a crowd – sliced cold ham does sandwiches and light meals for a couple of days. Dice any leftover ham and freeze it for 2–4 weeks only, then use it from frozen for adding to savoury sauces as pie filling, toss it with pasta or cook it with savoury flans.

HAMBURGERS
Store and use bought frozen hamburgers according to the manufacturer's instructions.

Home-made Hamburgers
Season fresh minced steak and pound the meat together so that it binds well. Shape into burgers and open-freeze (page 93), then wrap in cling film and pack in polythene.

Alternatively, mix about 50 g/2 oz fresh breadcrumbs, some chopped fresh herbs, seasoning and an egg with 450 g/1 lb minced beef. Shape into burgers and freeze as above.

Storage Time Up to 9 months.

Use Grill, bake or fry from frozen. Cook slowly until the outside is evenly browned and the meat cooked through.

HEADSPACE
When liquid freezes, it expands so when freezing sauces, soups, stocks, stews or other dishes which contain a good deal of liquid a little space should be left in the container. As a general guide, about 1–2.5 cm/½–1 inch space should be left between the food and the lid. In large, narrow, tall containers up to 3.5 cm/1¼ inches ought to be left.

HERBS
See butter (page 46) and bouquets garnis (page 43).

Freezing fresh herbs is an excellent way of preserving their flavour for times when they are not available. There are three accepted ways of freezing herbs:

Chopped   Parsley, tarragon, rosemary, mint, dill, chervil and coriander leaves are all examples of herbs that may be chopped and frozen in small packs or rigid containers.

Sprig or Leaves   Thyme, savory, sage leaves, bay leaves and basil leaves may all be frozen whole. When frozen the leaves are brittle and they may be crushed or crumbled. The tiny leaves on thyme or savory come off easily while the sprigs are frozen.

Herb Cubes   Chopped herbs may be frozen with some water in ice-cube trays, then packed in polythene bags. The cubes may be added to stews, sauces and so on. Make sure there is plenty of the chopped herb in each ice cube and note the quantity on the label. The disadvantage of this method is that the dish will be slightly watered down.

Storage Time   About 6–9 months.

FREEZER TIPS   Some of the stronger herbs – for example, bay leaves – can dominate a delicate chicken dish if they are used in quantity and frozen for long periods. When used in minced beef dishes the strength of the bay leaves is not as noticeable. Remove herb sprigs and bouquets garnis when the food has cooled, before freezing.

HORSERADISH

Fresh horseradish freezes well.

Preparation   Scrub and trim the root, then peel and chop or grate it. A food processor is a great boon for this!

Pack   In rigid containers or polythene bags.

Storage Time   9–12 months.

Use   From frozen. Mix with soured cream or mayonnaise to make a sauce or dressing. It may also be added to savoury white sauces for serving with beef or fish (Polish style – delicious!).

I

ICE BOWLS

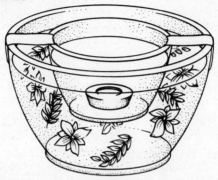

Make ice bowls for serving sorbets and ice creams. You need two freezer-proof bowls, one about 5–7.5 cm/2–3 inches smaller than the other. Chill the bowls and a large quantity of water. In the sink, half-fill the larger bowl with water. Place a weight in the smaller bowl and put it in the larger one. Use parcel or freezer tape to keep the smaller bowl floating in the middle of the large one. Put the bowls in the freezer. Push flowers and leaves down between the bowls before the water is frozen and leave until a bowl-shape of ice is formed. Individual bowls may be made in the same way. Untape the small bowl, then release the large one by rinsing the outside in warm water. Put the ice bowl back in the freezer until you are ready to serve the ice cream. Often ice bowls may be saved for use several times if the ice cream does not melt in them. Wipe out any smears of ice cream with damp absorbent kitchen paper.

ICE CREAM

Make 600 ml/1 pint thick custard: either use 4 egg yolks, 25 g/1 oz cornflour, 25 g/1 oz caster sugar and 1 teaspoon natural vanilla essence or use 3 eggs and 3 yolks,

25 g/1 oz caster sugar and 1 teaspoon natural vanilla essence. If using cornflour the custard may be boiled; if using eggs and milk alone the custard must be cooked in a bowl over a pan of hot water until thickened. Cover the surface of the custard with cling film and cool.

Whip 300ml/½ pint double cream with 25 g/1 oz icing sugar until it stands in soft peaks. Fold this cream into the custard, then freeze the mixture. When half frozen (after about 4–5 hours) thoroughly beat the mixture. Freeze and whisk once or twice more. Then replace in the freezer until firm. The more often the mixture is beaten, the smoother the ice cream, as this process breaks down the ice crystals.

Flavouring Ice Cream

Fruit purées may be folded into the custard before the cream. About 300 ml/½ pint strongly flavoured fruit purée is sufficient and the vanilla should be omitted. If the fruit is tart, the purée should be sweetened. If the flavour is delicate, more purée should be added. The flavour of the fruit should be quite strong as it will be more delicate when frozen.

Coffee essence, melted chocolate or cocoa dissolved in boiling water, brandy, rum or liqueurs may be added to the cooked custard. Chopped nuts, chocolate chips or grated chocolate, diced fruit, dried fruit soaked in alcohol or a little chopped mint should be mixed in after the final beating.

Storage Time   Home-made ice cream will only freeze well for 1–2 months. After that ice crystals begin to develop and the mixture tastes grainy.

Serving   Allow the ice cream to stand in the refrigerator for about 20 minutes to soften slightly before serving.

ICE CUBES

For parties, make lots of ice cubes in advance and store them in polythene bags. Or make super-cubes by freezing water in clean yogurt cartons – they are ideal for adding to punch as they do not melt as quickly.

Flavour ice cubes with concentrated fruit juice, squash or cordial. Good in fizzy lemonade or mineral water! For more sophisticated drinks add grated orange or lemon rind to the water when making cubes. Set small pieces of lemon or orange rind, stuffed green olives or cherries in individual ice-cube holes.

INSURANCE
See page 19.

J

JAM-MAKING
Frozen fruit may be used to make traditional jam. During freezing the pectin content is slightly diminished. Fruits which contain plenty of pectin (apples, black-currant, redcurrants, crab apples and marmalade oranges) will still give a good set after freezing. Those with a medium content (raspberries, plums and apricots) should be mixed with some fresh fruit or with a little apple pulp to make jam. About an extra eighth of the weight should be added in fresh fruit. Fruit with a low pectin content (rhubarb and strawberries) should be cooked with about a quarter of their weight in apple pulp for a reasonable set.

JELLY
Like gelatine, this does not hold a good set during freezing and thawing.

K

KIDNEYS
May be frozen for short periods and only if really fresh.
Preparation   Trim off all the fat, halve and remove the cores.

Storage Time Up to 2 months.
Use Cook from frozen. Make sure grilled or fried kidneys are cooked through.

KIPPER
See smoked fish (page 114).

KIWI FRUIT
See fruit (page 70).

L

LABELLING
Always label packs of food before freezing.

LEEKS
May be frozen for use in cooked dishes such as stews or sauces.
Preparation Remove the outer leaves and trim off the ends. Slice thickly and wash thoroughly, then drain well.
Blanch For 2 minutes. Alternatively, quickly sauté the slices in oil or butter and cool.
Pack In usable amounts.
Storage Time Up to 9 months if blanched; 6 months if sautéed.
Use Quickly fry from frozen for adding to casseroles, soups, sauces and other cooked dishes. Sautéed leeks may be added straight to assembled casseroles.

LEMONS
Whole or prepared lemons may be frozen for making marmalade. The grated rind and juice may be frozen together in ice-cube trays, then packed, ready for use in sweet or savoury dishes. The grated or finely shredded rind may be frozen separately from the juice.
FREEZER TIP Open-freeze (page 93) lemon slices, then pack. Add straight to drinks.

LIMES
As for lemons (page 82).

LIVER
When absolutely fresh, liver may be frozen for short periods.
Preparation   Trim, remove any outer membrane. Cut into slices, if wished.
Pack   Individual pieces in cling film or pack in usable weights.
Storage Time   Up to 2 months.
Use   Place in a dish and thaw in the refrigerator for several hours or overnight. Drain, rinse in cold water and pat dry on absorbent kitchen paper.

LOBSTER
A live lobster may be killed by placing it in a large polythene bag, or clean carrier bag, in the freezer. This

is considered to be a humane method of killing. Leave the lobster in the freezer for 5–6 hours or until frozen. Cook from frozen.

Cooked lobster is best frozen as prepared meat in a wine or Béchamel sauce.

Bought frozen cooked lobsters should be thawed and prepared according to the manufacturer's instructions. They are usually frozen in water.

LOGANBERRIES

These freeze very well and are a good 'pick-your-own' fruit.

Preparation Lightly rinse the fruit in small batches, then drain on absorbent kitchen paper.

Pack Open-freeze (page 93) before packing in polythene bags. This prevents crushing as well as providing free-flow packs.

Storage Time Up to 1 year.

Use Use from frozen, saving all juices.

LOLLIPOPS

Remember that lollipops taken straight from a home-freezer are very cold and they can stick to wet lips.

Follow the manufacturer's instructions for bought lollipops. Make home-made ones in special moulds. Use concentrated fruit juice, squash or cordial diluted with water. Instead of moulds, fill individual yogurt cartons and place sticks in them, then freeze.

FREEZER TIP For no-fuss lollies, simply plunge wide sticks straight into a carton of fruit yogurt and freeze. They are fun to eat and a good way of steering young children away from very sweet treats.

LYCHEES

Fresh lychees may be frozen in syrup.

Preparation Make a cut into the skin around the fruit, then remove the skin. Slit the opaque flesh down one

side and carefully slide out the large stone.
Pack In light or medium syrup (page 118) in rigid containers.
Storage Time Up to 1 year.
Use From frozen. Mix with other fruits in salads or cocktails.

M

MACKEREL
See fish (page 67).

MANGE-TOUT
Freeze well for use in cooked dishes but not for salads.
Preparation Top and tail the mange-tout, wash and drain.
Blanch For 2 minutes.
Pack Open–freeze (page 93), then pack.
Use Straight from frozen. Best quickly stir-fried in a little oil or butter, or with other ingredients in an oriental stir-fry. Alternatively, plunge into boiling water and cook for about 2–3 minutes, until thawed and hot. Drain and serve at once.

MANGOES
See fruit (page 70).

MARGARINE
Place packs of block margarine in a polythene bag and seal before freezing. Tubs may be frozen as they are – if the lids are insecure, then seal with freezer tape.
Storage Time Up to 6 months.
Use Thaw in the refrigerator overnight.

MARROW
Marrow which has been frozen tends to be rather watery and soft on thawing – better to make a large batch of chutney!

MAYONNAISE
This will not freeze successfully – the eggs and oil separate and curdle.

MEAT
See also bacon (page 36), sausages (page 113) and hamburgers (page 77).

The fat content of meat is important in determining the storage life as it tends to go rancid. A high salt content (for example in cured meat) combined with fat, as in bacon, reduces the freezer life dramatically. Follow these general guidelines for all meats along with the storage times suggested below.

Joints   These should be trimmed and neatly trussed in shape ready for cooking. Wrap an awkward-shaped joint in heavy-duty foil, then in polythene and extract air from the bag before sealing.

Do not stuff joints before freezing. If you intend cooking the meat with a stuffing, then bone it and freeze it neatly flattened so that it will thaw quickly.

Steaks and Chops   Trim off excess fat before freezing. Wrap these individually in cling film, then pack them in polythene.

Cubes   Open-freeze (page 93), then seal in polythene bags for free-flow packs.

Minced Meat   Open-freeze (page 93) spread out on a tray, then break the mince into small pieces and pack in a polythene bag. A polythene tube (page 21) may be used to pack portions of mince in a long string, sealing between each portion with a metal tie.

Strips   Cut thin slices of tender meat across the grain, then cut into fine strips. Open-freeze (page 93) these and pack. A few may be removed at a time for making stir-fries and, if they are cut fine enough, they may be cooked quickly from frozen.

Packing   Good packing is essential for meat, otherwise the lean will dry out and suffer from freezer burn (page 69) and the fat will become rancid. Heavy-gauge polythene should be used and it is best to wrap the meat first in cling film or foil.

Freezing Quantities of Meat   Make sure that you freeze only the weight of meat suggested by the freezer manufacturer and always use the fast-freeze setting.

If you are buying meat in large quantities ready for freezing, consider the type of cuts and the ways in which you intend using them, also your requirements in terms of quantity. If you are a family of six you will need far more than if there are just two of you.

Storage Time

Beef – About 9–10 months (the shorter time for fattier cuts).

Veal – Up to 9 months.

Lamb – About 6–9 months (the shorter time for fattier cuts).

Pork – About 6–9 months (lean cubes or steaks stay in better condition longer).

Use   Thaw meat before cooking, the exceptions being free-flow mince and fine strips which may be cooked from frozen. Thaw the meat in the refrigerator overnight or for several hours in the case of small cuts. Make sure that the meat is in a container which will not allow it to drip on other foods and that it is placed near the bottom of the refrigerator. Discard the drips, rinse the meat under cold water and pat dry on absorbent kitchen paper.

FREEZER TIP   By far the best way of buying meat for freezing is from a small, good butcher who provides special bulk packs of mixed or selected cuts. Look for a butcher who will freeze the meat for you, then transport it home rapidly.

MERINGUES

These freeze well. Pack individual meringue shells or small meringues in a rigid container. Large circles of meringue or cases may be frozen with care but considering the difficulties of preventing damage to such fragile foods, it is best only for a few weeks.

Storage Time Up to 6 months in an airtight container.

Use Fill or sandwich together while frozen; ready to eat almost immediately, certainly within 1 hour.

MICROWAVE

The microwave is a natural partner for the freezer as it does provide a fairly speedy means of thawing food. There are a few rules to observe both for safety in use of the appliance and for food safety.

☆ Always read and follow the microwave manufacturer's instructions. If you lose these, contact the manufacturer for a new set.

☆ Do not use metal containers or implements in the microwave.

☆ Generally, when thawing food use the Defrost or Low setting.

☆ Unwrap food to be thawed, place it in a suitable container and cover it.

☆ Check the food occasionally as it thaws. Turn pieces of food over, separate items that are frozen in a block or break up blocks of stew, sauce or soup.

☆ Observe standing times suggested by the manufacturer, particularly when thawing large or dense items such as meat or poultry.

☆ Before increasing the setting to cook large items, make sure they are thawed through. Check meat and poultry to ensure that it is thawed before cooking.

☆ When thawing and reheating certain items in one operation be sure that all the food is thoroughly reheated before serving. This method may be applied to sauces, some casseroles and minced meat dishes.

☆ If in doubt, buy a thermometer designed for checking the temperature in the middle of food and cooked dishes.

☆ When thawing bread, cakes or similar, stand them on double-thick absorbent kitchen paper to absorb any excess moisture.

☆ Cheese may be thawed in the microwave but take great care not to overheat it and cause areas to melt.

☆ Some delicate items, such as cheese or butter, may be part-thawed in the microwave, then left at room temperature to thaw completely.

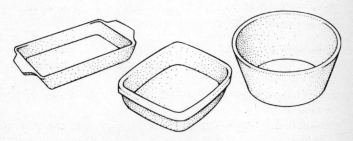

Freezer-to-Microwave Packing

If you use the microwave for thawing food, take this into account when you are packing food for freezing. For example, an irritating mistake I have made is to pack soup in very tall containers, then the frozen block is too tall to fit in the microwave.

There are several ranges of containers that are made to go from freezer to microwave. Remember that you can always line the dish with cling film before putting the food in it for freezing, then remove the block of food and pack it for storage. Discard the cling film before returning the food to the dish for thawing.

Boil-in-the-bag packs are useful for thawing and heating in the microwave, especially when storing individual portions. Always place the pack on a plate or dish and pierce it before putting in the microwave. Use microwave-proof ties for sealing bags that are to go into the microwave.

Thaw foods in plastic containers for 1–2 minutes in the microwave on a Defrost setting so that the block of food will slip easily from container to dish. Never force a lid off a plastic container which is taken from the freezer as the lid may break. Instead heat it in the microwave on a Low setting for 1–2 minutes.

MILK
See goat's milk (page 74).

Homogenized milk freezes well, ordinary or skimmed milk becomes grainy on thawing. Do not freeze milk in bottles. Waxed cartons may be frozen.
Storage Time   Up to 1 month.
Use   Thaw overnight in the refrigerator.

MUSHROOMS
Although frozen mushrooms are useful for flavouring if you do not have any fresh ones, they cannot be compared texture-wise with fresh ones.
Preparation   Quickly rinse button mushrooms and trim their stalk ends. Rinse open mushrooms holding their caps uppermost under running water for a few seconds. Shake off the water and trim the stalks. Button mushrooms may be frozen whole but I prefer to slice all mushrooms for freezing as their softened texture is less noticeable. Very small button mushrooms are worth freezing whole.
Blanch   Do not blanch in water but toss the prepared mushrooms briefly in hot butter or oil over a fairly high heat.
Pack   In usable amounts in small rigid containers or bags. Label with the weight of raw mushrooms.
Storage Time   3–6 months, depending on whether

butter or oil was used.

Use   No need to thaw: heat the mushrooms in a pan or add them to dishes. Use the mushrooms and their liquid for making roux-based sauces.

MUSSELS

Cooked mussels freeze quite well in their liquor for adding to dishes on thawing.

Preparation   Prepare and cook the mussels in the usual way – scrub and scrape the shells, remove the beards and discard any open shells. Cook in a little liquid – white wine, dry cider or water – with some seasoning, chopped shallot or onion, parsley and a little lemon rind. Shake the covered pan over a high heat for a few minutes until all the shells are opened. Discard any shells that are closed.

Shell the mussels and place them in a container. Strain the cooking liquid over them and cool before freezing.

Storage Time   About 2–3 months.

Use   Part-thaw the mussels in the refrigerator for a few hours, then add them to sauces, seafood casseroles and risottos (about 5–10 minutes before the rice is cooked).

N

NUTRIENTS

Correct preparation and blanching is important to retain nutrients before freezing. Food should be absolutely fresh; fruit and vegetables should be frozen soon after picking. Vegetables should be prepared, blanched, packed and frozen speedily in one operation.

The blanching (page 41) period must be accurately timed and the cooling process should be as rapid as possible. This results in the minimum seepage of nutrients into the blanching and cooling water.

Correct packing is also important to prevent nutrient loss. Also rapid freezing, using the fast-freeze setting, will help to retain nutrients by minimizing any damage to the structure of the food. On thawing, there is some unavoidable loss to drip (page 63) from meat but this is not extensive if the food is frozen quickly. Cooking frozen vegetables rapidly in the minimum of water and for short periods is important to retain nutrients.

NUTS

Whole nuts may be frozen in their shells. When fresh brazils, almonds, pecans and so on are available, freeze some for cracking open later. They keep well for 6–9 months.

O

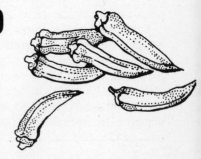

OKRA

Frozen okra is best suited to longer cooking in casseroles (gumbo or spiced Indian-style braised dishes) as it becomes soggy on thawing.

OLIVES

Halved or roughly chopped olives may be frozen for use in cooked dishes (for example pasta sauces) or to sprinkle over pizza.

ONIONS

Onions are not worth freezing, apart from small pickling onions which are useful for adding to stews.
Preparation Peel and leave whole.
Blanch For 3–4 minutes.
Pack Double-pack to prevent their odour escaping.
Use From frozen.

OPEN-FREEZE

This is the term used for freezing food before packing it. The food is spread out on trays lined with cling film or foil and placed in the freezer until firm. It is then packed in bags and sealed.

This method provides free-flow packs of vegetables, so that small amounts can be removed as required. It also prevents delicate fruits and foods from being crushed. Open-freezing is also useful for foods such as fish fillets which can be kept in a good shape.

ORANGES

Fresh sweet oranges are available all the year round so there is no reason to freeze them. Seville oranges, used for making marmalade, are only available for a few weeks early in the year and are well worth freezing.

Either freeze the whole fruit, then thaw it and prepare marmalade in the usual way or cook the fruit and freeze it ready for boiling with sugar at a later date. This is particularly useful if you want to make chunky marmalade and if you have a pressure cooker. The fruit can be cut up and cooked quickly in a pressure cooker, cooled and frozen. The more time-consuming process of boiling with sugar and bottling can be carried out at leisure.

Remember to label the packs with the weight of fruit. The whole fruit will keep well for 6–9 months, the cooked for up to 1 year.

FREEZER TIP Freshly squeezed orange juice and grated rind can be frozen together or separately.

P

PACKING FOOD
See freezing equipment and packing materials (pages 20 and 21).

Adequate packing is probably the most important part of the preparation of food for freezing. The packing must form essential protection against cross-contamination between frozen food (both flavour and potential bacterial contamination), dehydration, loss of flavour, possible oxidation (which causes rancidity) and damage.

Food which is inadequately packed dries out on the surface, a condition known as freezer burn (page 69). Fats (page 66) which are exposed to air will turn rancid more quickly and any food which has a distinct flavour will taint other freezer contents if the packing allows this. Also, bacteria present in food may be transferred to other items if flimsy packs are torn and foods are mixed.

Foods must be packed in hygienic conditions. The packing materials should be stored in a clean place. Bags should be kept in a closed outer covering; cling film in a closed box or dispenser and rigid containers should be washed and dried before packing food.

Different types of food should always be kept separate. For example, if you are freezing chicken portions and peas, the two should be prepared and packed separately, with thorough cleaning of utensils and surfaces in between. Small amounts of different foods (wrapped in cling film, perhaps) should not be combined in the same polythene bag.

Excluding Air

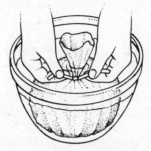

To keep the food in best condition, as much air as possible should be removed from bags. The habit of placing a drinking straw in the opening and sucking air out is not to be recommended because it is not hygienic.

An alternative method is to submerge the pack in a bowl of cold water, keeping the open end well above the level of the liquid. The water surrounding the pack will push out the air. The end of the pack should be sealed with a wire tie just below the water level. Then the outside of the pack should be dried. This is a messy process but it does work.

Better still, buy a cheap vacuum pump (page 25).

Double-Packing

For anything that is strongly flavoured. Use two sets of outer wrapping material or place a sealed polythene bag in an airtight rigid container.

PANCAKES

These freeze well unfilled. Filled pancakes may also be frozen but the texture of the pancakes does soften on thawing and reheating. So it is better to freeze pancakes and filling separately.

Preparation   Layer absorbent kitchen paper between the pancakes when they are cooked. Leave to cool.

Pack   Interleave the pancakes with cling film or freezer film, then pack them in a large polythene bag.

Storage Time   Up to 3 months.

Use   Remove the number of pancakes required. Placed individually on absorbent kitchen paper, they thaw very quickly at room temperature. Remember to keep the pancakes covered as they thaw.

Heat a little butter and oil in a pan, then quickly reheat the pancakes, turning each one once. If they are to be filled, simply divide the filling between them and roll or fold before heating them in the oven.

PARFAIT

A parfait is a rich ice cream, made with lots of whipped cream, possibly with confectioner's custard added.

Rum and Orange Parfait

Stir 100 g/4 oz icing sugar into 450 ml/¾ pint double cream. Add 6 tablespoons rum and the grated rind and juice of ½ orange. Whip the mixture until thick, then pour it into a freezer container and freeze overnight. The parfait is usually soft enough to serve straight from the freezer.

Substitute brandy, sherry or any liqueur for the rum, using only 75 g/3 oz icing sugar with sweetened liqueurs. The orange rind and juice may be omitted.

PARSNIPS

These freeze well when cooked and mashed. They discolour if frozen raw and they are soft if frozen cooked in chunks. It is best to par-boil them and add them to stews after thawing to finish cooking.

PASSION FRUIT
See fruit (page 70).

PASTA
Cooked pasta shapes do not freeze well as they tend to be soft, with a grainy texture, on thawing. However, stuffed and layered pasta dishes do freeze successfully. Lasagne, cannelloni or ravioli in sauce may be frozen cooked. Uncooked stuffed pasta shapes, such as ravioli or tortellini, freeze well. Storage time is about 2 months, depending on the fillings or sauces used.

Bought fresh pasta is an excellent freezer stand-by. It may be stored for 2–3 months and cooked from frozen. Make sure that any stuffing is cooked through before serving. Tagliatelle takes only a couple of minutes longer than normal to cook from frozen once the water is brought back to the boil.

PASTRY
See choux pastry (page 57), dumplings (page 64) filo pastry (page 67) and flans (page 69).

Pastry freezes well both raw and cooked.

Uncooked
Short Crust Pastry   Freeze it at the stage when the fat is rubbed into the flour, before adding any liquid. Pack the crumbs in a bag or rigid container and label with the quantities. Thaw in the refrigerator overnight or for a few hours at room temperature. The mixture may be worked from a part-frozen state.

Alternatively, the pastry may be frozen in a neat block once it is ready for rolling out. Wrap it in cling film and place in a polythene bag.

Storage Time   Up to 3 months.

Puff, Flaky and Rough Puff   Freeze when prepared and ready to roll out. Wrap in cling film and place in a polythene bag. Thaw in the refrigerator overnight or for several hours.

Storage Time   Up to 3 months.
Hot Water Crust   This should be shaped and filled before freezing if it is uncooked.
Storage Time   Up to 3 months, depending on filling.
FREEZER TIP   When freezing raw pastry, shape it into a neat, thin block which will thaw evenly and fairly quickly. Note the weight of pastry on the label. Do not freeze blocks which are too large to be thawed and used in one baking session.

Cooked Pastries

Cooked pastry dishes may be stored for 1–2 months, or up to 3 months for short crust. However, this depends entirely on the filling or other ingredients used.

Cooked puff, rough puff and flaky pastries are very fragile and they are difficult to store. Also, on pies and other filled dishes which are quite moist, the layers tend to collapse on thawing so the result is not as good as when freshly cooked. Cooked oblongs of puff pastry (for example, for making mille feuille) freeze well for short periods if they are packed in foil or a rigid container.

Before serving, cooked pastry items benefit from being crisped in the oven.

PATE

Generally I find that frozen pâtés are disappointing. On thawing they tend to be watery, therefore I do not recommend freezing them.

PEACHES

These may be frozen in syrup for later use in trifles or puddings. However, I think pieces of fruit are better stored in brandy or vodka, with sugar added to taste. When peaches are cheap, they make good chutney too. A purée of peaches with some lemon juice is a good freezer stand-by for making mousses, ice creams (page 79), or sauces (page 112).

PEAS

Along with canned salmon, bought frozen peas have become more popular than the equivalent fresh food. If you use a lot of frozen peas it makes sense to buy large packs. However, freshly picked peas freeze very well and they retain more of the fresh flavour than bought peas.

Preparation   Freeze peas on the same day as picking and select only tender young, plump pods. Shell them. From every 450/g/1 lb pods you will get about 225–275 g/8–10 oz.

Blanch   For 1–2 minutes.

Pack   In polythene bags.

Use   Cook from frozen, allowing about 5 minutes once the water has come back to the boil.

Sugar Snap Peas

These are half-way between peas and mange-tout. Both pod and contents may be eaten; unlike mange-tout there are tiny peas in the pods. They are sweet, tender and delicious. Excellent freezer candidates if you grow your own or pick them from a farm.

Preparation   Trim the stalk ends off the pods and wash well.

Blanch   For 1–2 minutes.

Pack   Open-freeze (page 93), then pack in polythene bags.

Use   From frozen, adding to boiling water. Cook for about 5 minutes once the water returns to the boil.

FREEZER TIP   Pea pods may be used to make surprisingly good white wine or to flavour soup. If you do not have time to make a large quantity of soup, or to brew up some wine, when you have finished freezing the peas, then wash and dry the pods and freeze them for up to a week, until you can use them.

PECTIN

See jam-making (page 81).

The pectin content of fruit depends on the type and the ripeness. Under-ripe fruit contains more than fruit which is ripened. The pectin content is diminished slightly during freezing but it is not completely destroyed.

If you want to freeze fruit for making jams or set preserves at a later date, then select a good proportion of slightly under-ripe fruit and freeze it as soon as possible after picking. Combine frozen fruit with some fresh fruit, or pectin stock.

Pectin Stock

Pectin stock is made by cooking and sieving apples. The 'stock' is then combined with fruit which do not naturally contain much pectin to give a good set when making jam. Although the pectin stock will not be as strong on thawing as when freshly made, it will still give a good set if used more generously than usual.

There is no need to peel and core all the apples for pectin stock. Trim any bad or bruised areas off the apples (windfalls are ideal) and cut them into quarters. Place in a saucepan with just enough water to cover. All sorts of apples may be used but the juice of 1–2 lemons ought to be added if using just eating apples. Bring to the boil, then simmer the apples for about 1 hour, slightly longer for eating apples, until they are pulpy. Cool the apples, then press them through a sieve. Pour the stock into rigid containers – freezing in quantities of about 600 ml/1 pint is a good idea. The larger the volume of pectin stock added to fruit for making jam, the firmer the set. As a guide, adding about 600 ml/1 pint stock (thawed) to 1.8 kg/4 lb fresh strawberries when making jam will give a set.

Leave the stock to thaw overnight in the refrigerator, then add it to the fruit once it has been cooked until soft (before adding the sugar).

PEPPERS

As well as the familiar green and red sweet peppers, occasionally yellow, orange, purple or even white ones are available. They freeze well for use in cooked dishes, although they are not suitable for use raw once thawed.

Preparation   Halve the peppers and remove all the core, stalk and seeds. Rinse the pieces of pepper well and dry them on absorbent kitchen paper. Cut the flesh into strips, then across into dice.

Packing   Either wrap small amounts in cling film, then place the small sachets in a polythene bag, or for free-flow diced peppers, line a tray with cling film and spread out the diced peppers in a thinnish layer. Cover and freeze. When hard, break up the layer of peppers and pack in polythene bags.

Use   From frozen. Sauté them as usual, with onions if used, for adding to casseroles, pasta dishes or other cooked dishes.

FREEZER TIP   Dicing is by far the best method of preparing peppers for freezing as the skin becomes more pronounced on larger pieces or strips. This is because the flesh tends to soften.

PET FOOD

Freezing is an ideal method of storing home-cooked pet food. Occasionally, I boil up some kidneys, liver, heart or other offal until tender, then add some fish until it's just cooked. Chopped, cooled and packed in small tubs (old glacé cherry tubs are ideal). Put all the tubs together in a polythene bag and label it clearly.

The freezer may also be used for storing fresh meat and other foods sold specifically for feeding to pets. In this case it is **vital** to make sure that the meat is well packed, then double-wrapped in bags that are immediately identifiable – coloured striped large storage bags, for example. Muddling pet food with other stores may seem unlikely but it *must be avoided* as raw meat sold for pets should not be allowed to contaminate other food.

PIES AND TARTS

I think of pies as being made in a deep dish, usually without a pastry base. Double-crust pies have a pastry base as well as a lid. Tarts are shallow, made on tart plates or in a shallow tin, with a base and a lid. For the purposes of freezing information given here, open fruit tarts should be treated as flans. Pies and tarts may be frozen raw or cooked.

Uncooked

☆ Remember that the filling will take some time to thaw through and cook. Meat pies (and other pies with savoury fillings that require lengthy cooking) are better frozen with a cooked filling and uncooked pastry.

☆ Brush a little melted butter over the pastry base and allow it to set before adding the cooled filling. This makes a thin barrier between the pastry and filling to prevent it soaking in during freezing and thawing.

☆ Toss raw fruit with a little cornflour as well as sugar before putting it in a double-crust pie or tart. This thickens juices which run from the fruit as it cooks, preventing the pastry base from becoming soggy.

☆ Deep pies should be thawed in the refrigerator overnight. Place a piece of absorbent kitchen paper over the pastry lid and stand the pie dish in a baking tin to catch any condensation which may drip from the outside of the dish.

☆ Glaze the pastry after thawing.

Cooked

☆ Cooked fruit pies made with short crust pastry are an excellent freezer stand-by.

☆ Be sure to use a dish that will withstand the low temperature in the freezer (enamelled plates are great – but not for microwave thawing).

☆ The pastry should be very slightly underbrowned when the pie is cooked.

☆ Thoroughly cool and chill the cooked pie before freezing.

☆ Wrap puff pastry pies very carefully to avoid cracking the crust.

☆ Thaw the pie overnight in the refrigerator or for several hours at room temperature.

☆ Make certain that pies to be served hot are thoroughly reheated before serving, particularly the filling in the middle.

☆ Even if the pie is to be served cold, the pastry benefits from crisping in a hot oven just before it is served. If the filling is warmed and allowed to stand, it provides the ideal environment for micro-organisms to multiply and this can cause food poisoning (meat and poultry pies in particular).

FREEZER TIP   Cooked individual pies with fairly solid fillings are ideal for packed lunches. Make them in deep patty tins. Fillings such as sausagemeat, spinach and cheese mixtures or spicy bean mixtures are suitable. Small pies removed from the freezer in the morning will be thawed by lunch time.

PINEAPPLE

Fresh pineapple is worth freezing for short periods when it is ripe and cheap.

Preparation   Trim the ends off the fruit, peel it and cut out all the spines. Halve the flesh, cut out the core, then cut the rest of the fruit into chunks or dice.

Pack   In rigid containers in syrup (page 118).
Storage Time   About 3–4 months.
Use   Thaw in the refrigerator overnight or at room temperature for several hours. Use in trifles and other desserts. The fruit may be used for filling a flan: drain off the thawed syrup and thicken it with arrowroot to use as a glaze.

PITTA BREAD
Look out for mini pitta, wholemeal pitta and (best of all, I think) the thick, round, two-thirds-cooked pitta that are very similar to the real thing sold wrapped around skewered meat in Greek slouvaki pitta. All types freeze well and may be heated from frozen under a grill, in the microwave, on a barbecue or in a hot oven.
Storage Time   Up to 3 months.

PIZZA
The best way to freeze pizza is to do so when the base is part-cooked and not topped. Fully cooked pizza may be frozen, thawed and heated but the result is not as good. Authentic Italian pizza should be made on a thin yeast-dough base but similar savoury dishes can be made on bought bases or on a scone base.

PLUMS
These freeze well for use in cooked dishes – pies, crumbles or other baked puddings. Frozen plum purée is ideal for making fools, mousses or soufflés.
Preparation   Wash, dry and stone the fruit. The easiest way to remove the stones is to cut round each plum, then twist the halves apart.
Pack   In polythene bags, sprinkled with a little sugar or the plum halves may be packed in syrup (page 118).
Storage Time   Up to 1 year.
Use   Cook from frozen. The thawed plums tend to be rather mushy.

POTATOES

Do not freeze raw or part-cooked potatoes. Cooked new potatoes may be frozen but they are watery and unpalatable when thawed. Similarly, part-cooked chips may be frozen but they are not worth the effort involved. Fully baked potatoes may be frozen, then thawed and heated in one go until hot through and crisp outside. They are not bad but they do taste reheated. However, it is useful to remember if you have a pile of baked potatoes left after a barbecue party.

Cooked mashed potato freezes well. It should be thawed for several hours at room temperature, then beaten well before being used as a topping for cottage pie. To serve plain, the mashed potato may be reheated in a covered dish in a steamer, in the microwave or it may be sprinkled with some grated cheese and baked until golden.

Roast potatoes freeze reasonably well, ready for thawing and heating in the microwave or oven.

By far the best freezer candidates are prepared potato dishes – croquettes made simply by coating buttery mashed potato in egg and breadcrumbs; or layers of sliced potatoes and onions baked together until tender and golden. Here is one of my favourite freezer recipes for potatoes.

Potato Pancakes

Peel and coarsely grate 900 g/2 lb potatoes. Rinse the grated potato under cold running water, then squeeze it well to remove the liquid. Mix in 50 g/2 oz plain flour and 2 eggs. Add plenty of salt and pepper. If you like, add some chopped fresh parsley, a crushed garlic clove and a few tablespoons of chopped black olives.

Heat a little oil in a frying pan and drop in spoonfuls of the potato mixture. Flatten the mixture into fairly thin round cakes and fry them over a medium heat until they are golden underneath. Turn the cakes and cook the second sides until crisp and golden. Drain on absorbent kitchen paper and cool.

Stir the mixture each time you take a spoonful to add to the pan, otherwise the flour and egg tend to separate slightly from the grated potato.

When cold, pack the cakes in a polythene bag, interleaving them with film.

Storage Time   About 3–4 months.

Use   Reheat from frozen, either in a little hot oil, under the grill or in the microwave. Make sure they are thawed and hot through before serving.

POWER CUTS
See In an Emergency (page 18).

PRAWNS
Bought frozen prawns are useful for making all sorts of instant meals. When buying look at the quality of the prawns – some sold as 'cooking prawns' are small, broken, tough and leathery. The majority of ready-frozen prawns are sold cooked and peeled. When buying loose prawns do not freeze them unless you are sure they have not previously been frozen – most fishmongers sell thawed frozen prawns loose. Small brown shrimps, freshly caught and cooked in fishing ports, are worth freezing.

Frozen large, raw Mediterranean prawns (king prawns) are sold by good fishmongers or some specialist stores. They are ideal for making seafood kebabs or superior seafood dishes, such as paella.

Q

QUICHES
See flans (page 69).

Traditional egg and milk fillings for quiches are not at their best when frozen and thawed but they are acceptable as a quick supper. Adding a little cornflour gives a result that is not as light but which is not watery when thawed. Try this basic freezer recipe.

Set the oven at 200°C/400°F/gas 6. Line a 25 cm/10 inch flan tin with short crust pastry and prick it all over. Place a sheet of greaseproof paper in the pastry case, fill with baking beans and bake for 20 minutes.

Cook a chopped onion in a little oil or butter until soft. Gradually stir a little milk taken from 300 ml/½ pint into 25 g/1 oz cornflour. When smooth, beat in 3 eggs, then beat in the remaining milk. Add seasoning and beat well.

Sprinkle the onion in the flan case. Add 100 g/4 oz grated Gruyère cheese and some chopped parsley. Pour in the egg mixture and bake for 40–50 minutes, until set and golden. Cool.

To freeze, remove the quiche from the tin. Either freeze it whole or cut it into slices and wrap each in cling film, then pack in a rigid container.

Storage Time About 2 months.

Use Thaw a whole quiche in the refrigerator for several hours, then reheat it in the oven before serving. Individual slices usually reheat quickly and successfully from frozen.

R

RASPBERRIES

These freeze and keep extremely well and they make wonderful trifle.

Preparation The fruit should be just ripe, large and just firm (not squashy). Rinse small batches of fruit very briefly and dry them on absorbent kitchen paper. Open-freeze (page 93) before packing in polythene bags or rigid containers.

Storage Time   Up to 1 year, or longer.

Use   Use from frozen. For trifles, I sprinkle the frozen fruit over a sponge base, then add a little icing sugar and warm custard. By the time the custard has cooled and chilled, the fruit is just right.

REDCURRANTS

Redcurrants are the perfect freezer food – they have a short season and are difficult to find at other times.

Preparation   String the currants, rinse them and dry them on absorbent kitchen paper.

Pack   In small packs – they do not usually form a solid block unless they are overripe.

Storage Time   Up to 1 year, or longer.

Use   Use from frozen.

REHEATING FOOD

There are certain standards that we all ought to think about when reheating food that has been frozen and thawed (in fact, exactly the same applies to any food which has been cooked and cooled). The reason for concern over proper reheating of food is because of micro-organisms which may cause food poisoning.

Micro-organisms are minute living organisms that are present all around us. They include bacteria, yeasts and moulds. The majority are destroyed by boiling but there are some which produce spores that can withstand ordinary cooking. Given that good hygiene standards are observed, there is no need to become neurotic about micro-organisms. In their 'normal' presence they do not cause problems. Foods such as poultry that contain salmonella-producing bacteria must be cooked through to destroy the particular bacteria.

When food is frozen the micro-organisms are dormant. For example, food does not become mouldy. It is important to remember that when food thaws, the micro-organisms that were present before freezing gradually become active again. This means that they multiply. The temperature of the food plays a role in determining how quickly the micro-organisms multiply. Bacteria are most active between 21–35°C/70–95°F. For this reason, food should be kept cool while it is thawing.

Here are a few guidelines for dealing with frozen cooked dishes.

☆ Food which is frozen in rigid covered containers should be left in them to thaw.
☆ Packs of food should be unwrapped and placed in covered dishes or the whole pack should be left closed and placed in a dish to catch any drip (page 63).
☆ Either put the food in a refrigerator or in a cool room to thaw.
☆ Never leave food uncovered while it thaws.
☆ When the food is thawed it may be reheated. Stews, sauces and similar dishes should be stirred before reheating.
☆ The food should be removed from the freezer, thawed and reheated fairly quickly. Once thawed the food should be used on the same day. For example, something that is thawed overnight in the refrigerator should be reheated and used next day.
☆ Do not reheat food at too high a temperature so that it becomes overcooked outside while still cold in the middle.
☆ Stews, sauces and so on should be stirred during reheating. Small items should be turned over to ensure even reheating.
☆ The important point to remember is that all the food should be reheated to the original cooking temperature. Pay particular attention to large pieces of meat or poultry in casseroles or in sauce; cottage pies; pie fillings; fillings or layers in pasta dishes and so on.

Thoroughly reheating the food destroys the bacteria.

☆ Reheating food from frozen is not usually recommended because of the risk that the middle of the food may not be thoroughly reheated. However, stews and other moist dishes that do not dry out easily may be reheated from frozen. The dish should be covered and it must stand up to the combination of frozen food and heat. The food **must** be heated slowly in the oven or on the hob (more difficult) until it is thawed and bubbling hot in the middle.

☆ Always check that the food is hot through, then serve it swiftly – do not leave it uncovered on a work surface before serving.

RHUBARB

Freezes very well. Select only tender young stalks.

Preparation   Trim the stalks and peel off any tough outer strings. Cut into slices.

Pack   Either open-freeze (page 93) and pack in large bags or pack in usable quantities.

Storage Time   Rhubarb keeps well for up to 1 year.

Use   Cook rhubarb from frozen.

FREEZER TIP   Both rhubarb purée and stewed rhubarb freeze well. When cooled, pack the cooked fruit or purée in rigid containers.

RICE

Most supermarkets and freezer centres sell a variety of cooked rice products, from plain rice to rice mixtures. Follow the manufacturer's instructions for reheating and using the products. Home-cooked rice which is frozen and thawed can be disappointing. Freezing is ideal for any leftover cooked rice; however on thawing the grains can be rather soft and 'grainy'.

FREEZER TIP   When making risottos or rice mixtures, undercook them slightly for freezing. Avoid adding ingredients which do not freeze well (for example, do not add hard-boiled eggs to kedgeree). It is best to thaw more complicated rice mixtures before reheating them.

ROSES
Perfect rose flowers and buds may be frozen for later use in an arrangement but they do not last well when thawed. Individual petals may be open-frozen (page 93), then packed in a rigid container for use in cooking.

ROYAL ICING
Royal-iced cakes do not freeze well. The icing keeps well without freezing if kept clean and dry. Cakes covered with sugarpaste (page 118) may be frozen.

S

SALADS
Salad vegetables do not freeze well as they become limp and rather slimy or very soft on thawing.

Salad dressings do not freeze well; mayonnaise separates as does a vinaigrette (there is no reason to freeze this anyway).

SALMON
Salmon may be frozen whole, cut into steaks or in fillet portions.

Preparation Whole salmon should be gutted and descaled. Make sure that a large fish will fit into the freezer – no problem in a chest type but there may not be enough room in an upright freezer to lay the fish flat. If there is not enough room to keep a whole fish flat, then it may be curved in a large flan dish. The fish should be prepared as for cooking before it is frozen.

Packing Wrap the fish in cling film before packing it in polythene bags or foil.

Storage Time   Up to 3 months. As salmon is an oily fish, the fat may go rancid if stored for too long.
Use   Thaw the fish in the refrigerator overnight.

SANDWICHES

Depending on the type of filling, sandwiches can be frozen successfully. Making a batch at the weekend and freezing them for taking for packed lunches can be a good idea.

FREEZER TIP   Frozen sandwiches may be toasted without thawing. Set a sandwich toaster to medium heat or lower a rack under the grill to make sure that the filling is heated through.

SAUCES

Some sauces freeze well, others do not. Pack the sauce in a rigid container or in a container lined with a polythene bag. Thaw the sauce in the refrigerator or at room temperature in a covered container. Most sauces should be whisked well and reheated gently.

Roux Sauces   Thickened with flour cooked in fat. May be made of milk (Béchamel sauce, cheese sauce), stock (gravy) or wine. These freeze well but they must be whisked thoroughly on thawing and once or twice during heating. Do not be put off if the sauce looks slightly separated when it is thawed – it will become smooth when whisked and heated.

Cornflour Sauces   These freeze reasonably well but they tend to be thinner on thawing than when originally cooked. The same applies to custard sauce made with custard powder.

Sauces Thickened with Egg   These must not be frozen as they curdle and cannot be rescued. Set or pouring custard and other sauces that are enriched with egg yolks come into this category.

Cream Sauces   Sauces with cream added should not

be frozen as they curdle. The cream may be added after thawing and reheating.

SAUSAGES

Buy ready-frozen sausages and follow the manufacturer's recommended storage instructions. Some butchers will freeze a batch of their own make of sausages for you. I also take advantage of the opportunity of freezing any unusual finds in the way of specialist sausages. Only freeze sausages that are absolutely fresh. When buying from a butcher, check that they are made just before you buy them if you want to freeze them.

Preparation Either arrange the sausages in neat quantities ready for use or snip the links into individual sausages.

Packing Sausages may be open-frozen (page 93) before packing or bundles of the required quantity may be wrapped in cling film before putting in a polythene bag.

Storage Time 3–4 months. Remember that most have a high fat content, therefore they may go rancid with prolonged storage.

Use It is absolutely essential that sausages are cooked through before they are eaten. For this reason it is usual to recommend that they should be thawed in the refrigerator or in a cool place before cooking.

SHORT-TERM FREEZING

Freezing is also a useful method of storing particular items in the short term. For example, you may pick enough fresh peas for two or three meals, in which case some can be frozen for up to 2 weeks without blanching.

Using the freezer when planning dinner parties makes particularly good sense. Soups (page 116), pastry dishes (page 97), casseroles (page 49) and gâteaux (page 74) may be prepared a few days in advance and frozen. If you are an ambitious cook, do not dismiss the freezer in favour of many hours of complicated preparation before a meal; instead, think ahead and prepare stocks, sauce bases, make fresh pasta, sieve fruit purées, whisk up meringues and so on. Using the freezer in this way allows more time for creating special meals.

When food is to be stored for short periods, it may be packed accordingly. For example, a gâteau which is to be frozen for 2 days may be tented with foil. However, take care to prevent strong odours and flavours from contaminating other foods. If you pack something very lightly for short-term storage, then decide to leave it in the freezer for a longer period, remember to over-pack the food, exclude as much air as possible and seal it properly.

SMOKED FISH

Smoked Fish to be Cooked
Smoked haddock, cod, coley and kippers may all be frozen in boilable bags or roasting bags ready for cooking. Add a pat of butter to each pack. Use microwave-proof ties if you intend cooking the fish in the microwave. As well as simmering in boiling water, this type of pack may be placed in a steamer.
Storage Time   Up to 3 months.
Use   The fish may be cooked from frozen.

Ready-to-serve Smoked fish
Smoked salmon, trout and mackerel may also be frozen successfully. Leave the fish in vacuum packs or wrap fillets in cling film before placing in a polythene bag. Smoked salmon offcuts are a good freezer stand-by for making delicious pasta dishes quickly. Open-freeze (page 93) the offcuts before packing, so they can be cooked from frozen.
Storage Time   About 2–3 months.
Use   Thaw the fish in the refrigerator for several hours.

SORBETS

It really is worth taking advantage of owning a freezer to make sorbets or water ices, parfaits (page 96) and ice creams (page 79). A sorbet is a frozen, flavoured syrup. To achieve a smooth result, the sorbet must be whisked or beaten at least once, if not more, while it freezes. This breaks down the ice crystals. Once the mixture is smooth, the sorbet should be allowed to freeze until firm. Before use, it should be left in the refrigerator for about 15 minutes until it is just soft enough to scoop. When the sorbet has melted very slightly, the flavours will also be more noticeable.

Gelatine or Egg Whites Gelatine may be added to a sorbet mixture before freezing or whisked egg whites may be folded into the part-frozen mixture when it is whisked to break down the ice crystals. These are added to promote a smooth result and, in the case of egg white, so that the sorbet does not freeze too hard. They are not essential ingredients and a better result may be achieved by whisking the sorbet at least twice during freezing. This is easy if you own a food processor or ice cream maker but an arm-aching task if you have to work by hand.

Syrup A heavy syrup is used for making sorbet. The mixture relies on the sugar concentration to give the smooth, slightly soft result. The less sugar used, the harder the result. If a lighter syrup is used, then the sorbet should be whisked more often or an egg white or gelatine should be added. Remember, too, that the mixtures which seem oversweet before freezing taste less so when frozen.

Flavouring Fruit is the main ingredient used to flavour sorbets. Citrus rind, fruit juices and purées may all be used. The mixture should have a good strong flavour before freezing as this will not be as pronounced when the sorbet is frozen.

Lemon Sorbet

Place the grated rind and juice of 3 lemons in a large
saucepan. Add 225 g/8 oz sugar and 600 ml/l pint water.
Heat until the sugar dissolves, then bring to the boil and
boil, uncovered, for 5 minutes. Leave to cool. If
preferred, the lemon rind may be pared in strips and
cooked in the syrup, then removed before the mixture
is frozen.

Pour the syrup into a freezer container, cover and
freeze until the syrup is firm all around the edge and
underneath. Chill a bowl and whisk (an electric beater is
best or food processor bowl and blade). Whisk the
sorbet mixture until smooth. Return it to the freezer and
leave until half-frozen, then whisk again until smooth.
Freeze until firm. Place in the refrigerator for 15
minutes before serving.

SOUP

Being able to freeze home-made soup is one of the real
boons of owning a freezer.

☆ Smooth soups freeze best – leek and potato (vichy-
   soisse), tomato, cauliflower, lentil, pea, onion, carrot
   and so on.
☆ When freezing chunky soups, only part-cook any
   added vegetables. By the time they are thawed and
   thoroughly reheated they will be tender.
☆ Puréed soups are best frozen in their thickest state.
   For example, cook vegetables and some stock, then
   purée and freeze the mixture. Add extra stock or any
   milk used in the recipe to the thawed, heated soup to
   thin it to the required consistency. This saves on both
   freezer space and thawing time.
☆ Never add cream, yogurt, fromage frais or eggs to
   soup before freezing. They will curdle on thawing.
   Add them after the soup has been brought back to
   boiling point and cooled slightly.
☆ Leave the final seasoning until after the soup has
   been thawed and reheated.

SPICES

Highly spiced dishes are best used within about 2–3 months, otherwise the spices may dominate the thawed dish. However, the result does depend on the combination of ingredients used and how well the spices are balanced by other flavours.

Freezing is also a useful method of storing certain spices or spice combinations. Whole spices, such as cardamoms or juniper berries, are worth freezing. Keep them in small airtight containers in a sealed polythene bag to prevent their flavour or odour from escaping. They may be used from frozen.

Fresh Ginger

Fresh root ginger may be frozen. Trim and peel the root, then cut it into very fine strips and pack them in a small airtight container. Alternatively, trim fairly young root ginger, rinse and dry it, then coarsely grate it. Discard the last chunk of skin. Wrap small quantities of the grated ginger in pieces of cling film, then place them in a polythene bag.

Lemon Spice Paste

A paste of fresh root ginger, garlic, and lemon is a versatile flavouring. If you have a food processor or blender, making a large batch is easier than messing about with small quantities. Purée the grated rind and juice of 2 large lemons with 100 g/4 oz peeled fresh root ginger and 4–8 garlic cloves. Divide into four small portions and wrap in cling film. Pack the four pouches in a small airtight container in a polythene bag. The paste may be used to flavour fish, poultry or meat. It may be combined with soy sauce and spring onions in Chinese-style dishes. It forms a basis for cooking Indian-style, adding ground coriander (or chopped fresh coriander leaves), cumin, turmeric, chilli powder and ground fenugreek. It may also be combined with ingredients such as honey to make an excellent marinade for chicken.

STEW
See casseroles (page 49).

STOCK
Make stock from chicken bones, beef marrow bones or fish trimmings. Simply simmer the bones in a covered pan with a quartered onion, a bay leaf, a couple of parsley sprigs, a carrot and a celery stick, both cut into chunks, for about 2 hours. Do not season the stock – it is better to season the dish or sauce in which it is used.

For freezing, boil the cooled strained stock until it is reduced to about a third of its original volume. Freeze it in usable batches. On thawing, the stock should be thinned with water to its original consistency. Concentrated stock may be frozen in ice-cube trays so that the cubes can be used for making small quantities of sauce or for flavouring dishes.

SUGARPASTE
Cakes covered with sugarpaste may be frozen for up to 3 months. This is particularly useful when covering and decorating a light cake, such as Madeira cake. Pack the sugarpaste-covered cake in a large rigid container before adding any final decorations. Thaw it overnight in the refrigerator, then add piped decorations or other finishing touches.

SWEDES
Not really worth freezing raw or plain boiled but cooked mashed swedes freeze well.

SYRUP
Syrup may be used for packing some fruit in rigid containers when freezing. The syrup acts as a barrier between the fruit and air, helping to prevent discoloration and to maintain the quality of the fruit over long periods. In the early years of freezing, a great fuss was

made of packing fruit with sugar or syrup; however, for most fruit plain packing is quite adequate. Packing in syrup is useful for fruits such as peaches, pineapple, apricots or other dessert fruits which may be thawed and used without further cooking.

The strength of syrup is a matter for personal taste. A medium strength syrup may be made by dissolving 350 g/12 oz sugar in 600 ml/1 pint water and bringing the syrup to the boil. For a lighter syrup use 225 g/8 oz sugar. Heavy syrup may be made by increasing the sugar to 450 g/1 lb but this does tend to mask the flavour of the fruit.

Make the syrup several hours in advance, leave it to cool, then chill it before use, ideally overnight in the refrigerator. The cooler it is when put into the freezer, the quicker the fruit will freeze and the better the result. Never add fruit to hot syrup unless you particularly want to cook the fruit.

For fruits which discolour very easily, some lemon juice or ascorbic acid (page 34) may be added to the syrup. As a guide, the strained juice of 1 lemon or 400 mg ascorbic acid should be added just before use to 300 ml/½ pint syrup to help prevent discoloration.

Allow about 300 ml/½ pint syrup for 450 g/1 lb fruit. The fruit should be packed in a rigid container and only enough syrup used to cover the pieces of fruit. There should be about 1–2.5 cm/½–1 inch headspace (page 77) in the container. Place some lightly crumpled greaseproof paper on top of the fruit before putting the lid on the container – this will help to keep the fruit submerged in the syrup.

T

TEMPERATURE GUIDE

Domestic freezers should have an internal temperature of −18°C/0°F or lower. This is the temperature level at which frozen food may be stored safely without deteriorating over recommended storage periods.

Fast-freeze Setting

Also known as 'super-freeze' setting. This over-rides the thermostat to keep the motor running for longer periods and therefore reduce the internal temperature of the freezer and its contents. This is important when freezing a large quantity of fresh food. Always follow the manufacturer's instructions. The faster the food is frozen, the better it will be on thawing. The water content of the food will freeze into small ice crystals causing less cell damage. In turn this reduces the loss of moisture by drip (page 63) as well as during storage.

Star Rating

Always check that a freezer is marked with a four–star rating, showing a single star separated from three stars.

 This indicates that the appliance will reach and maintain a temperature low enough for freezing food and for prolonged storage of frozen foods.

A three-star rated freezing compartment is suitable for storing commercially frozen food for up to 3 months and it will maintain a temperature of −18°C/0°F. However, fresh food should not be frozen in this type of compartment.

The two-star rating is used for compartments which run at a temperature of −12°C/10°F. These may only be used for storing commercially frozen food for up to 1 month.

The one-star rating is used for compartments

which operate at −6°C/21°F. Commercially frozen food may be stored at this temperature for up to 1 week.

Storing Purchased Frozen Food
Look on packets of purchased frozen foods to find instructions relating to the star-marking system.

THAWING FOOD
Correct thawing is just as important from the point of view of quality and food hygiene as the way in which food is prepared before freezing. There are two main reasons for thawing foods which are subsequently cooked: to ensure that the food is thoroughly cooked through when it is served; to give the best cooked results, avoiding the possibility of overcooking certain areas before others are thawed and cooked.

Of course, some foods are not cooked after they are thawed and in these cases careful thawing is even more important. Ideally, foods should be thawed slowly, in the refrigerator. When handling meat, poultry, fish and other protein foods or cooked dishes that require long thawing, this is most important to avoid any risk of bacteria multiplying and causing food poisoning. However, under the proper conditions, food may be thawed in a cool room.

Whether at room temperature or in the refrigerator, the food should always be placed in a covered container. Generally, the food should be removed from the freezer pack (some items in rigid containers may be left in the container). Meat or poultry should be placed on a rack in a dish so it does not sit in the freezer drip (page 63). Failing this, the drip should be drained away during thawing.

Items such as small cakes, breads, some pastries and pieces of cheese are best thawed on a double-thick layer of absorbent kitchen paper on a plate. The whole plate should be covered.

When leaving food to thaw, particularly at room temperature, check it occasionally and always cook it or transfer it to a cooking dish or clean container when it has thawed. Food which has been thawed at room temperature should be placed in the refrigerator if it is not cooked immediately.

When preparing bought frozen food, always read and follow the manufacturer's instructions. Their advice is intended to give the best-quality, safe results so do not ignore it.

Thawing in the Microwave
See microwave (page 88).

Always follow the manufacturer's instructions for the choice of setting and the recommended time. When thawing commercially prepared products, check any instructions for microwave thawing or cooking on the packet and follow them closely.

All metal ties and packing should be removed from frozen food before thawing it in the microwave. The food should be placed in a suitable container and, usually, it should be covered. During thawing the food should be turned, stirred or rearranged for even results.

Always observe recommended standing times when thawing food. The standing time allows the temperature of the food to become even throughout.

THERMOMETER
A freezer thermometer is an inexpensive and practical accessory, allowing you to check that the internal temperature of the freezer is as low as it ought to be. If it is not low enough, the setting should be adjusted and the temperature checked.

Some freezers are now available with built-in thermometers.

TOMATOES
Do not freeze whole, as they collapse. They freeze well

as purée (sieved to remove seeds and skin), sauce or soup.

TRANSPORTING FROZEN FOOD
Always make sure that frozen food is not allowed to thaw while taking from the shop freezer to the home freezer. When buying frozen food along with other foods, always select the frozen items last. Never leave frozen food (or any food, for that matter) in a warm car while doing other errands. These notes may be of some help.

☆ Pack frozen foods and other chilled items in an insulated bag (or chiller bag).
☆ If you do not have a chiller bag, pack all frozen items neatly together in a polythene bag or polythene carrier bag. Keeping them in a 'block' helps to keep the cold in. If possible wrap the whole pack in newspaper and place in a cardboard box.
☆ Put the shopping in the coolest part of the car.
☆ Unpack frozen foods immediately you return home and place them in the freezer at once.

TURKEY
Uncooked turkey freezes well but care must be taken to ensure that only really fresh birds are frozen, that they freeze quickly and that they are properly thawed and cooked before serving. Before Christmas, many country turkey farms sell free-range birds and they are ideal freezer candidates.

Cuts of Turkey Turkey is available in many forms, either fresh or ready-frozen. Look out for turkey fillets cut from the breast meat. These may be cut into slivers, cubed or beaten out flat before freezing. Some butchers sell whole boneless turkey breasts ready-frozen.

Preparation If you are freezing a large whole bird, then make sure that you have the space in the freezer, also that the fast-freeze setting (page 120) is used according to the manufacturer's instructions. Beforehand, check that you have a large, suitable freezer bag. If you intend storing the turkey for any length of time, then wrap it first in cling film, then place it in a bag.

Remove the giblets from the bird and trim off the wing and leg ends. Cut off any lumps of fat from just inside the body cavity and singe away any remnants of feathers. Check that the turkey is properly cleaned inside, with no signs of tubes or other innards. Rinse the inside of the bird under really cold running water, then pat it all dry with absorbent kitchen paper. Truss the turkey, wrap it and remove all the air.

An excellent way of freezing turkey is in halves or quarters. Use poultry shears, a meat cleaver or a heavy chef's knife to cut the bird in half down the back. Cut through the breast bone to separate the two halves. Each half may be cut across in two portions, one with the wing and most of the breast meat, the second with the leg and some breast meat. Cut away any small pieces of bone before packing each portion of turkey.

Alternatively, the drumsticks may be removed and frozen separately; or the wings and drumsticks may be frozen apart from the main carcass.

Pack In strong bags, excluding as much air as possible, ideally using a vacuum pump (page 25). It is important that the packing is strong and that air is excluded to prevent any fat on the bird from going rancid.

Storage Time Up to 9 months.

Use Be sure to take the bird out of the freezer in time for it to thaw properly before cooking. Also check that you have sufficient refrigerator space to keep the turkey cool as it thaws. As a guide, a turkey weighing about 2.75 kg/6 lb will take 2 days to thaw in the refrigerator. A bird weighing 4.5 kg/10 lb will take 2–3 days and a 6.75 kg/15 lb bird will require 3–4 days.

The frozen turkey should be placed in a large dish

and then covered. Keep the turkey covered tightly with cling film and drain off any drip (page 63) which collects in the container. Make sure that the bird does not drip outside the container. Thawing turkey portions takes less time but the same technique should be used.

Make sure that the turkey has thawed before it is cooked – this is to avoid the possibility of any thick areas of meat being undercooked at the end of roasting. FREEZER TIP Never stuff a turkey before freezing it. Similarly, never stuff a turkey until just before it is to be put in the oven. If you do stuff the body cavity of a bird, make sure it is thoroughly cleaned, rinsed and dried first. Cook a stuffed bird slowly until it is thoroughly cooked through – remember undercooked stuffing in the middle of a bird can harbour bacteria that cause food poisoning.

W – Z

WATER ICE
See sorbet (page 115).

YEAST
Fresh yeast freezes very well. It may be purchased from bakers who still bake on the premises. Also, some hot-bread counters in supermarkets.
Pack Pack the yeast in 15–25 g/½–1 oz quantities, wrapping each portion in cling film. Put the individual portions in a polythene bag and freeze.
Storage Time About 3–4 months.
Use Small packs of yeast usually soften after about 15–30 minutes at room temperature. Then combine them with the warm liquid and sugar (if used) and leave to become frothy as usual.

YOGURT

Most cartons of fruit yogurt have a note on them recommending that the contents are not frozen. In fact, sweetened fruit yogurts do freeze reasonably well, although they may be slightly watery on thawing. Ready-frozen yogurts are available – these are specially produced for freezing and thawing without separating.

Unsweetened plain yogurt should not be frozen as it tends to separate becoming either curdled or very watery on thawing.

Yogurt Fruit Freeze

Yogurt may be used to make a tangy ice cream equivalent. Try this quick recipe. Stir 100 g/4 oz icing sugar into 450 ml/¾ pint fruit purée. Fold in 450 ml/¾ pint plain yogurt and freeze. Beat well until smooth when about two-thirds frozen, then freeze until firm.

THE FAMILY MATTERS SERIES